LIVERPOOL
JOHN MOORES UNIVERSITY
AVRIL ROBARTS LRC
TITHEBARN STREET
LIVERPOOL L2 2ER
TEL. 0151 231 4022

Changing
PLACES

Children's Participation in
Environmental Planning

WITHDRAWN

D1312951

LIVERPOOL JMU LIBRARY

3 1111 00783 3260

LIVERPOOL
JOHN MOORES UNIVERSITY
AVRIL ROBARTS LRC
TITHEBARN STREET
LIVERPOOL L2 2ER
TEL. 0151 231 4022

Changing
PLACES

Children's Participation in Environmental Planning

EILEEN ADAMS & SUE INGHAM

PLANNING AID
for
LONDON

Providing Free & Independent
Town Planning Advice

The
Children's
Society

A Voluntary Society of The Church of England and The Church in Wales

© Eileen Adams and Sue Ingham 1998

All rights reserved. No part of this publication
may be reproduced, stored on a retrieval system,
or transmitted in any form, or by any means, electronic,
mechanical, photocopying, recording or otherwise
without the prior permission of the publisher.

First published in 1998

The Children's Society
Edward Rudolf House
Margery Street
London WC1X 0JL

A catalogue record of this book is available from
The British Library.

ISBN 1 899783 00 8

Eileen Adams and Sue Ingham have asserted their right
under the Copyright, Designs and Patents Act 1988 to be
identified as authors of this work.

Contents

Foreword

Anyone who has ever worked with children, or indeed any parent, knows that young people have an unnerving ability to ask deceptively simple questions. Questions that force you to re-evaluate suddenly things you'd long taken for granted. Children have a creativity untempered by adult restrictions and an ability to combine idealism with boundless energy and enthusiasm. So it's surprising that we haven't yet learned to make better use of these qualities. This book exploring the theory and practice of children's participation in environmental planning is a bold and welcome step in the right direction.

One of the ways children learn about themselves is through understanding the relationship they have with their surroundings. They are eager to see themselves reflected in the world around them. So it's easy to understand why they often have strong opinions about both the built and natural environment. It seems ironic then that they're often an unheard voice when planning decisions are being made.

More and more organisations have woken up to the need to promote a dialogue with the communities they serve. It's a logical move – only when development plans are informed by the needs and values of the majority are they truly sustainable. No planning department can afford simply to pay lip-service to the notion of public participation: the need to involve communities is now written into our planning legislation. And of course in simple economic terms, community involvement is an invaluable source of free advice and information.

However logical the arguments sound, there's no denying that getting children involved takes time and effort. Fortunately, this book offers tested strategies and insights into how to start and maintain that process. It's an investment that pays both short and long-term dividends. As well as helping tailor the built environment to the needs of individual communities, the educational benefits are equally profound. Through contributing to environmental planning, children can start to develop their critical and analytical skills – and gain their first experiences of making decisions that reflect varied and conflicting interests.

Even more importantly, they learn that they need not sit back and watch the world changing around them, but can play a part in helping shape the changes. I don't think it's too grand a claim that getting young people involved in co-operative decision-making helps develop their understanding of the principles of democracy, as well as the mechanics of participation.

I'm pleased to see an initiative being undertaken that encourages children to view themselves not as consumers, but as stakeholders. By involving them in environmental planning, we provide them with an opportunity both to think about and build the future. Not only is it a chance to consider what they want the environment to be like in the next millennium, it's also a way to develop skills that ensure that, when important decisions are being made, they can make their voices heard and play their part in determining the outcome.

ANGELA EAGLE MP
Parliamentary Under Secretary of State,
Department of the Environment,
Transport and the Regions

Preface

This book is written for planners, architects, landscape architects, community workers, youth workers and teachers. It will also be of interest to local government officers in housing departments, those who coordinate Agenda 21 initiatives, as well as elected members. It is addressed to housing associations and voluntary organisations as well as others with an interest in environmental education, regeneration initiatives or other kinds of environmental change. The aim is to highlight some of the ideas and experiences which support young people's participation in the planning process and to offer a framework for thinking and action.

The book has been commissioned by The Children's Society and Planning Aid for London. It is about how professionals can enable young people to engage in the process of planning for change, both changing attitudes towards the environment and changing the environment itself. It identifies adults who have worked with young people and explores the working relationships between them. It considers issues which have emerged from a variety of projects in different parts of the country, and describes strategies used to engage young people in the process of change. This book promotes the fundamental principle that children are the future and that their rights and expectations should be considered in planning.

The preliminary research on which the book is based was carried out by Planning Aid for London. Information was sought by means of a press release, a questionnaire to relevant organisations, a literature search and contact with The Children's Society's projects. Organisations consulted included community technical aid centres, local planning departments, voluntary organisations concerned with the environment, youth work projects, community arts groups, planning organisations, architects and children's charities. The press release, literature search and networking created further contacts who provided information and useful material. A return rate of 30 per cent to the questionnaire yielded 574 completed questionnaires, 320 of which contained examples of good practice and schemes where children had been involved. Of these, a number contained additional reference material from the organisations concerned. The questionnaires were analysed according to the methods of consultations used, geographical location and types of organisation. Further research was undertaken by the authors to select and investigate the projects that are documented. From various sources of information, 20 case studies have been included in this book to show how children and young people were engaged in the planning process in various kinds of projects.

Acknowledgements

Our thanks to all those who have contributed to the research:

Margaret Fennely, Council for Environmental Education; Kim Jackson, VOYCE, Brighton; Mike Parker, Devon Youth Council; Paul Eyres and Mike Jones, Liverpool 8 Children's Research Group; Martin White and Pauline Gardiner, Erdington Local Action Plan, Birmingham; Laura Troup, David Brinn and Jane Wright, Brecon Beacons National Park, Planning for Real; Michael Jeeves, Traffic Calming Project, Leicester; Jackie Naylor and Susan Francis, Patio Estate Consultation Project, Rotherham; Colin Whitehead and Anne Baldwin, Newbury Park School, Redbridge; Wayne Allen, Allerton Young People's Project, Bradford; Cathy Maund and Brenda Southerden, Godolphin Road Community Garden, Shepherds Bush, London; Cathy McCulloch, EcoCity, Craigmillar, Edinburgh; Sav Kyriacou, Hammersmith and Fulham Urban Studies Centre; Judith Crangle, Cambridge City Council Play and Recreation Department; Chris Freeman, Cambridge City Council Community Development Department; Lynn Connor and Mick Nightingale, Islington Park Renovation Project, Salford; Helen Thomas, Kingston University; David Stone, Islington Schools Environment Project; Janet Eccles, Gillespie Primary School, London.

Our thanks also to those who contributed substantially to the ideas or the writing:

Julian Agyeman for the initial outline; Angela Anthony for the initial research; Ken Baynes for his inspirational work on design education; Ruth Barker and Joan Kean for the report on Newcastle Architecture Workshop; Liz Court for the report on Community Design for Gwent; Bill Lucas for the material on Learning through Landscapes; Bob Mayo for the advice on the youth service; Steven Ruse for the report on Setting up a Youth Forum, Leeds; Colin Ward for his seminal work on environmental education and children's participation; Helen Woolley for the report on Futuretown research.

Our thanks to the following for the illustrations:

David Brinn, Brecon Beacons National Park (Figures 1 and 5); Newcastle Architecture Workshop (Figures 3, 14, 17 and 18); Pauline Gardiner, Osborne School, Birmingham (Figure 4). We have been unable to trace the copyright holder for Figure 10, but we will be happy to include an acknowledgement in future reprints.

The Children's Society would like to thank the members of the Publications Advisory Group for their valued advice: Kathy Aubeelack; Nicola Baboneau; Ron Chopping (Chair); Sara Fielden; Nicola Grove; Virginia Johnstone.

Introduction

As we approach the millennium, we sense the uncertainty of the future, but acknowledge the inevitability of change. How do we anticipate change in the environment, visualise it and make it real? Planning is essentially about relationships between people and place. It is about shaping and managing the environment. It is about a sensible and appropriate use of resources. It is about dealing with change. It is about having a vision of the future. But this cannot become a reality unless it is a shared vision of what needs to be done.

In a democratic society, we have government by consent. Why not planning by consensus? This would involve all those affected by environmental change, including young people. At present, what roles are young people assigned in relation to the environment – consumer or steward, passive victim or active citizen? How can they share in the planning process? Many young people have a passionate concern for the environment and want to play a positive role in shaping it. There are many benefits to be derived from encouraging their participation.

Where planners have involved young people in planning matters and enabled them to glimpse the design, economic and political processes which shape the environment, the result has been an increased understanding of the complexity of the planning process. Young people are then more appreciative of the challenge planners face and more aware of the problems and constraints inherent in dealing with change. They realise there are no easy solutions and that conflict and compromise are inevitable. They understand the impact that planning has on people's lives and realise that planning matters.

Planners benefit too. Young people provide them with a fresh perspective. They have an optimism and enthusiasm which is encouraging and motivating. Their questions can help planners perceive the environment afresh and their proposals provide insights as to what is important to young people.

Professionals say that they want an informed and critical public, arguing that this will result in improved professional practice and better environmental quality. But an articulate and environmentally literate public will only emerge if an investment is made in education for participation. This is an area where people learn primarily from experience. Their attitudes to planning and to the environment will reflect that experience, as victims or protagonists, consultees or collaborators.

The need is to develop new kinds of relationships where people feel a sense of involvement, a degree of ownership and a measure of control. They are then more likely to show concern and responsibility for their environment, resulting in more effective stewardship. Planners and others involved in environmental design and community development will find in this book guidance as to how to develop a shared vision with a critical public, which will benefit young people, professionals and the environment.

The ideas, examples and practical suggestions presented in this book represent an enormous amount of experience developed over many years. Readers are invited to build on this work to enable young people to engage in actions which can make a positive difference to themselves, to the environment and to the society in which they live. Those experienced in the field will welcome the clarification of the thinking that informs the work, set out in the context of current policies. Those eager to be involved but uncertain how to manage it will find both inspiration and practical guidance to enable young people to participate in the exciting process of dealing with change.

Part I of the book sketches in the context for young people's involvement in planning for environmental change. It identifies issues relating to children and young people, the environment and education, and makes a case for young people's participation in environmental planning.

Part II reports on a variety of initiatives where young people have been involved in making proposals for change, both changing people's attitudes to the environment and changing the environment itself. It explains how they have worked through the tasks they have set themselves, which will inspire others elsewhere.

Part III offers a framework for education for participation. It explains strategies that professionals can employ to help young people observe and analyse their environment, develop critical skills, develop design capability and communicate their ideas to others. It sets out in detail the practicalities and thinking involved in planning and organising projects with young people. This overall framework can be utilised by environmental and educational professionals in a variety of settings and developed into strategies for participation.

In this book, we use the words 'children', 'young people' and 'youth' to indicate people up to the age of 18. Specific ages are identified at the beginning of each case study.

THE CONTEXT FOR PARTICIPATION

Figure 1 Children in Gilwern School, Abergavenny, learn about planning (Case Study 7)

Part I sets out the background to children's involvement in environmental change. It looks at their concerns, and the local, national and international initiatives which affect their involvement. It also examines environmental education, both in a school context and in relation to community and environmental organisations. The nature, level and efficacy of children's participation in environmental planning is discussed.

CHAPTER 1 Children and young people

This chapter discusses the environmental issues that concern children, and their experience and perceptions of the environment. It also describes the policies already in place which support the participation of children and young people in the planning process.

United Nations Convention on the Rights of the Child

The United Nations Convention on the Rights of the Child (1990) sets out 54 articles which identify principles and standards for the treatment of children. By 1994, the Convention had been ratified by 154 countries, including the UK Government in 1991. Only 20 member countries of the UN have not ratified it. For the purposes of the Convention, a child means every human being below the age of 18 years.

Article 3 states that all actions concerning the child should take account of his or her best interests, whether undertaken by public or private social welfare institutions, courts of law, administrative authorities or legislative bodies.

Article 12 states that children have a right to express an opinion on all matters which concern them and their views should be taken into account in any matter or procedure affecting the child.

Article 15 states that children should have the right to meet with others, join and set up associations.

However, these requirements are not generally known, understood or accepted. Children and young people do not have the right to vote, nor do they have any formal way of making their views known or influencing political processes. How far are children visible in the environment? To what extent are they concerned about environmental issues? What policies are in place to support their involvement in environmental planning?

Access to the environment

Since Colin Ward (1978) wrote of children's experience of the environment and reported on their explorations of it, in the UK young people's freedom to explore and investigate the outdoor environment has been severely curtailed. Supervised and protected by adults in the family, at school and in the community, the environment over which they can exercise some personal choice and control is shrinking rapidly. Access to their locality is increasingly problematic, whether it is to play in the street, to travel on their own or to engage in community life. The 'bogeyman syndrome' is evident, where adults fear that children will be abducted or physically harmed when playing outdoors. Tightly structured schedules leave more affluent children with almost no time to themselves, and breaks in schools are becoming shorter as homework times lengthen. In western countries, the trend is towards commercial 'pay for play' centres, while in many other countries with emerging industries, children are being exploited as a labour force. With growing industrialisation and globalisation, children are losing contact with their local culture and becoming alienated from the natural environment (IPA Conference, 1996).

Adults' fears for children's safety and well-being are not unfounded. Meyer Hillman (1995) describes evidence of harm in a number of spheres of children's lives. He explains that children are increasingly suffering from respiratory and cardiovascular damage from vehicle exhaust pollutants and prospectively from insufficient opportunities for keeping fit by walking and cycling on a routine basis throughout childhood. They also run the risk of injury from the rise in the number, speed and acceleration of motor vehicles. Children are experiencing an erosion of rights because of parental restrictions on their independence outside the home in order to minimise risk. They are losing opportunities on the street and in the neighbourhood for acquiring practical and social skills from direct experience and for starting to play a role in community life.

This invisibility of children on the street and in the life of the community has implications for young people's participation in democratic processes. At the age of 18, we expect young people to adopt the rights and fulfil the responsibilities of active citizens, but how can they develop the skills and capabilities necessary to enable them to do so if direct experience of and involvement with their environment is becoming more and more restricted? Limited experience will create limited vision. Lack of opportunity for engagement will lead to lack of motivation to participate in the future.

Sense of place

Just as their experience of the environment differs from that of adults, so too do young people's perceptions. Their needs are different: they value places where there is evidence of inhabitation, of people and activity; they welcome the experience of feeling independent and being able to get around on their own;

they want more opportunities for play and social interaction; they want to be active, doing things, meeting people. Surprisingly, perhaps, they like things to be clean, safe and ordered. Their perceptions of risk and danger are also different from those of adults (Titman, 1994).

There is a link between young people's experiences and perceptions of their environment and the attitudes they develop towards it. Where children are able to establish a strong connection with a neighbourhood and develop a feeling of ownership and engagement with it, while at the same time feeling a sense of belonging, they can then develop a strong sense of place. This can only be based on first-hand physical, social and emotional experience, which is vital today when so much experience is second-hand and mediated, whether through programmed learning in school or the soap opera on the television. The fostering of a sense of place will work against feelings of dispossession and alienation.

What issues concern children and young people?

Whereas parents may be concerned about their children's education, health, safety and security, young people are not merely interested in their own personal well-being, but show a high degree of interest in global environmental issues and are often more knowledgeable and concerned than adults. *Rescue Mission Planet Earth: a children's edition of Agenda 21* (UNICEF, 1994) reveals the fears of young people from different countries about the differences between the rich and poor, consumerism, energy consumption, pollution, nuclear waste and desertification, alongside their hopes for changing lifestyles, better education, ecologically sound development, recycling and a new role for young people in changing the world. Young people are able to take an idealistic standpoint. They look to the future rather than to the past. They have expressed enthusiasm for learning about where they live and a real concern about the quality of life they will inherit.

Young people need experience of engaging with local issues to find out what is involved in attempting to resolve conflicts between different values, identifying alternatives and effecting change, before they can participate in solving the problems of the world. The issue of bullying is an example where children are taking steps to deal with an immediate social problem which has arisen in some schools and neighbourhoods. They are also concerned about environmental issues which can be tackled at local level. At a Roundtable organised for young people by the Local Government Management Board (1996), the issue of young people's lack of opportunity to influence change was raised. They were worried about transport issues, waste, pollution and litter; they wanted a safe and pleasant local environment, with appropriate space and facilities, but seemed uncertain about what they could do. Similar views have been expressed in other youth forums.

The Blueprint Findings (Leicester City Council, 1995) reports young people's views:

> Young people stressed the need for respect and opportunities. Whilst concern about issues like peace, disadvantage, pollution and discrimination were evident, many were sceptical about establishment institutions and felt marginalised from decision making. When combined with poor opportunities (for jobs, income and affordable things to do) an anti-authoritarian route to gaining money, 'kicks' and respect amongst peers was more likely to be fostered. Key points raised included:
>
> • Things to do need to be at affordable prices. Cinema, ten pin bowling, sports facilities, adventure playgrounds, youth clubs run by young people, motor tracks etc. are liked or desired.
>
> • Positive expressions of youth culture like music, dance and fashion should be promoted.
>
> • Opportunities for work and income (not 'exploitative training schemes') are needed.
>
> • Homelessness and problems faced by young people seeking housing are issues.
>
> • Respect, responsiveness to youth needs and the chance to take responsibility for their own actions and interests are important.

A voice

Young people need help to communicate their ideas and establish ways of sharing the decisions which affect their lives. At present, lobbies for the voice of the child to be heard tend to focus on child protection and welfare issues. There is also growing demand for a Minister for Children and a Children's Ombudsman. However, the danger is that this will create an emphasis on children as problems and childhood as an issue rather than engage young people positively in dealing with change. To include children themselves in change, a wider set of insights are needed. The idea behind planning is to use resources in the public interest, in an appropriate way for future needs. But how many local planning authorities have taken the UN resolution into account and make provision for children to be consulted about local planning issues that affect them, or ensure that their needs are fully considered when planning decisions are taken?

According to Save the Children, young people are most affected by changes to the environment, yet they are the people with the least voice: 'They play no part in the political system that determines the policies that affect them so tremendously. In fact, even when young people get to the age of adult status, millions feel so alienated and excluded that they do not even bother to vote' (White, 1996). Similarly, Ann Weyman, Director of Information and Public Affairs at the National Children's Bureau, states:

> We have a great deal to learn from young people where environmental issues are concerned, and we need to listen to their views. Their ideas and enthusiasm can make a significant contribution to the success of community initiatives aimed at improving the environment. Many local authorities and other organisations would be delighted to involve young people in environmental projects, but do not necessarily know the best way to go about it. (National Voluntary Council for Children's Play, 1995)

Children's participation can be promoted through existing structures with the help of inter-agency initiatives to enable young people to effect change from within their own organisations, though there may also be a need for new groups to evolve. Schools, play schemes and young people's organisations provide a ready-made focus and setting. Play is often used as a focus to link concerns about children's access to the environment, the provision of facilities for their physical and social development and children's rights. The National Voluntary Council for Children's Play (1995) advocates that 'Adults involved in children's play should aim to act as enablers to support and encourage the children's own ideas and decisions about what they do and how they do it, while safeguarding health and safety'. It recommends that a wide range of people, including children, should be consulted about planning for children: 'Children's provision should be planned with community involvement. Architects, planners and builders should work together with statutory, voluntary and private play service managers and workers, community and parents' groups, children and other relevant parties'.

It needs to be recognised that children can make a valuable contribution to the planning process, derived from experience of the environment and values which are different from those of adults. Their involvement can enrich the planning process as well as prepare them to play a more active role in shaping their environment as adults. But they cannot do it on their own without the help of adults in a variety of professional settings. In the next three chapters we look at the environmental and education policies which have the potential to promote young people's involvement in debate and action to improve the environment.

CHAPTER 2 Environment

This chapter describes the broader context for young people's participation in environmental change including the environmental, social and cultural issues which face them in the twenty-first century. It sets out the main national and international environmental initiatives, and discusses their implications for children.

Earth Summit 1992

The Earth Summit took place in Rio in 1992 with government representatives from 150 countries. It resulted in an Agenda 21 programme of action which integrated environment and development concerns aimed at preparing the world for the challenges of the twenty-first century. Concern focused on deteriorating environmental quality as a result of commercial exploitation and inappropriate environmental management, the danger of pollution from toxic chemicals and the management of waste products. The hope was for better provision to promote health and sustainable human settlements. It was agreed that 'By 1996 most local authorities in each country should have undertaken a consultative process with their population and achieved a consensus on a "local Agenda 21" for the community' (Jones, 1995).

Local Agenda 21

Central to the notion of Agenda 21 is the concept of 'sustainable development'. This is essentially about the quality of life, and includes concern for, among other things, consumption patterns, the distribution and use of resources, global economics and the protection of wildlife and their habitats. Agenda 21 is also concerned with people's involvement in decision-making about the use of resources, and their ability to take responsibility for ensuring environmental quality:

Each local authority has been urged to adopt its own individual Agenda 21, as a sustainable development strategy at local level, involving partnerships with sectors, such as businesses, community and voluntary groups. Central to Agenda 21 is the concept of participation – that communities and users of any kind of building or land, urban infrastructure, or public facilities, need to be involved in its development. (Community Architecture Education Group, 1996)

Following the establishment of Agenda 21, the Government has an obligation to consult young people:

The Agenda 21 agreement bound each country's government to set up ways to promote dialogue between young people and government at all levels, and to establish mechanisms that permit youth access to information and provide them with the opportunity to present their perspectives on government decisions, including the implementation of Agenda 21. (White, 1996)

Agenda 21 states that the creativity and ideals of young people should be mobilized in order to achieve sustainable development. Governments are urged to assist by promoting dialogue to facilitate young people's participation at local, regional and national levels (see Chapter 6 for Local Agenda 21 groups). Although raising awareness and developing dialogues are important, good intentions need to be translated into ideas which can be shared, developed and refined. What are our visions of the future? David Hicks (1994) takes the view that we need to develop a more future-oriented perspective to help young people understand the links between their personal lives and the wider issues of change: 'The images that we have of the future matter because they help determine our priorities in the present. Such images play a critical role in the creation of change. They exert a powerful influence over what people think is, or is not, worth doing in the present'.

The temptation may be to develop young people's awareness and concern about environmental issues and encourage them to voice complaints about environmental problems. It is more difficult for young people to visualise future or alternative possibilities. The need is to enable them to develop a positive view of change and a clearer vision of how things might be different to achieve a better quality of life for everyone. To be sustainable, this vision would have to include not only environmental protection, but also social participation. As the Community Architecture Education Group (1996) puts it: 'The rationale is simple: in a society with no common visions, only short-term decisions are made. Visions to be of value and to be realisable have to be shared by all: i.e. by experts and lay-people, by professions and building users. A non-participatory community is therefore inherently unsustainable'.

Habitat 2

These important links between environment, participation and children's rights were made at the Habitat 2 Seminar held in New York in 1996, articulating the environmental and social conditions necessary to address children's needs. Topics considered included the voice of the child, dialogue between children and adults, equal opportunities, children's environments, preparation for effective decision-making, community partnerships and mechanisms for children's participation in local government processes:

3.10. In recognition that democratic behaviour in a civil society must be learned through experience, children should be given a voice in their communities, according to their abilities. This will serve as a preparation for their full participation in civil society as adults and will be a means of better meeting their needs as children.

a) Basic education for children should include investigations and dialogue on local development and the local environment in order to facilitate participation for sustainable development.

b) In recognition of the marginalization of women in decision-making, attention should be given to preparing girls as well as boys with the confidence and skills to be involved as equal participants with their peers.

c) Children should be involved, according to their capacities, in the design of environments intended explicitly for them, such as play places, schools and children's hospitals.

7.1. Formal democratic mechanisms should be established for giving all citizens, including children, according to their capacities, a voice at the community and municipal level, both as a way of preparing for participation in civil society and as a way of improving the appropriateness and effectiveness of decision-making.

7.2 Children's participation works best in a society which also encourages adult participation; the participation of adults and children must be complementary and mutually reinforcing.

7.3 Local authorities should initiate the establishment of innovative partnerships between children, parents, schools, private sector and community-based organizations and NGOs to optimize the effectiveness of the existing structures by involving children in local community services provision. This will strengthen children's awareness and sense of belonging in the community.

7.4 Children should participate according to their abilities in the management of all institutions and facilities that they use, including schools, recreation facilities, children's organizations and community organizations.

7.5 Local government authorities should involve children, according to their capabilities, in local governance processes. (UNICEF, 1996)

These recommendations identify key points which need to inform young people's involvement in planning. Learning to participate can only take place through experience of the planning system and the support of a range of professionals and agencies.

Planning

Every few years, local councils, government departments, health and education authorities make proposals for planning and development. These cover everything from housing, transport and leisure, to workplace design, waste disposal and pollution control. Planning decisions affect everyone, including children. However, provision for the needs of children and young people does not feature prominently, and the way younger members of the community are included in consultation procedures varies widely.

Structure plans, addressing strategic policy issues, are prepared in counties, and a series of local plans are prepared by district councils, dealing with local level planning policies. Unitary authorities, which means London boroughs and metropolitan districts, and also newer authorities, need to prepare one plan which incorporates both wider strategic and local issues (Planning Policy Guidance, note 12, 1992). During the 1990s every borough in London began to prepare a unitary development plan (UDP). This acts as the framework for planning decisions, provides a basis for coordinating and promoting various developments and sets out various considerations when determining planning applications. It provides the basis on which all planning applications are negotiated and then determined. It is intended to protect existing community facilities and indicate where money needs to be spent. It helps local authorities consider the needs of particular groups such as disabled people, the black and ethnic minority communities, women, children and people on low incomes. It should guide public investment, both that of the council and other public bodies such as the National Health Service and transport authorities. It should guide and promote private investment to provide jobs, housing and shopping, and influence planning to improve and protect the quality of the physical environment.

In 1994, Planning Aid for London conducted a comprehensive review of the policies contained within each of London's 33 boroughs' UDPs to investigate how the needs of children had been incorporated into these plans, whether children were consulted or involved in the consultation process and how the policies reflected their needs. Although London based, the issues raised are national. The research reported that few UDPs consider children's issues seriously. However, it discovered that all the London boroughs had at least one policy that reflected the perceived needs of children in their area, concerned with, for instance, provision of amenity open space, childcare facilities in a variety of settings, nursery provision and play facilities (Planning Aid for London, 1994).

The views of children and young people could be counted as valuable information to guide the planning process. Through consultation, the development control system could provide a formal mechanism to make it possible for the voices of young people to be heard. Making the planning system more accessible and possibly the devolution of planning services could be ways to achieve this. There is increasing consensus on the problems of non-participation in the planning service. So there is a case for further research into how the planning system can facilitate participation, and perhaps a new planning policy guidance note is needed.

Regeneration initiatives

The process of regeneration works best if members of the local community are involved as consultees, participants and partners. They are, after all, the people whose lives and conditions are to be improved and who are the life of the locality. (See Chapter 9 for regeneration initiatives involving young people.) Recent guidance on regeneration (Department of the Environment, 1995) suggests pointers for success:

- If there is a tradition of self-help and voluntary action, a scheme which is aware of this and builds on this underlying energy is much more likely to succeed.

- A scheme which nurtures community involvement can add thousands of hours of people's freely given efforts to local development.

- Community involvement brings user feedback, enabling services to be better targeted and more effective.

- A scheme which has built up community involvement is more likely to be sustainable.

- Involving the community in a regeneration scheme is an opportunity to promote social cohesion and counter increasing fragmentation and alienation in everyday life.

Along with carers and retired people, children comprise a large group who are not in the labour market and who could make a strong contribution to community development. Although their energy may be channelled through voluntary organisations, and more often through community groups and networks, these are often overlooked because they are small and informal. The process of consultation is more likely to involve formally constituted groups and their representatives than children in smaller groups. The Community Development Foundation (1994) sums up the situation: 'People in communities have detailed knowledge of their own needs. However, people's ideas are not necessarily consistent. There are naturally many competing voices, and many more voices are not heard at all because people are not aware of the process or how to participate'. This reflects the experience of many children and young people.

CHAPTER 3 Education

This chapter describes the educational context for young people's participation in environmental planning and explains some of the influences which currently operate. It looks at environmental education, design and social education in schools, and their place within the National Curriculum. It also describes some of the environmental organisations which are concerned with education.

In recent years, the environment has come to be seen as an important educational resource, and has been used as both a focus and a context for study. Education *about, in, through* and *for* the environment has been part of government policy for a number of years now, first explained by Her Majesty's Inspectorate in 1981 (Department of Education and Science, 1981). Although in the last few years the main focus has been on the natural environment, concerns about the built environment have recently gained increasing importance. The Right Honourable John Gummer spoke in favour of young people's participation in environmental issues:

> What I want to emphasise is how invaluable the integration of the school into its local community can be. Schools are educating and training the future working population. And sustainable development pressures on these young people will not go away. We need to involve them in these issues now, and help them gain ownership of some of the solutions. (Department for Education and Department of the Environment, 1995)

Environmental education

In recent years, much has been done to promote environmental education in schools. *Teaching Environmental Matters through the National Curriculum* (School Curriculum and Assessment Authority (SCAA), 1996) offers guidance on the scope and purpose of environmental education in the National Curriculum, touches on management issues and makes reference to examples of work in schools. It clarifies the requirements of the National Curriculum in relation to environmental education and hints at some of the opportunities to develop this area of the curriculum. In environmental education, all the other school subjects can be utilised, including English, mathematics, science, geography, art, design technology, information technology, history, modern foreign languages, music, physical education and religious education. Environmental education aims to:

- provide all pupils with opportunities to acquire the knowledge, understanding and skills required to engage effectively with environmental issues, including those of sustainable development;

- encourage pupils to examine and interpret the environment from a variety of perspectives – physical, geographical, biological, sociological, economic, political, technological, historical, aesthetic, ethical and spiritual;

- arouse pupils' awareness and curiosity about the environment and encourage active participation in resolving environmental problems. (SCAA, 1996)

Advice by the School Curriculum and Assessment Authority is that:

- Education about the environment involves developing the sound base of knowledge, understanding and skills that pupils will need if they are to make sense of environmental issues.

- First-hand experience, or education in the environment, plays an essential part in learning. The experience can start in the school itself, in its grounds and immediate locality, progressing to activities in more distant, contrasting localities. The environment at first-hand and through secondary sources, also provides stimulus for learning a wide range of skills – education through the environment.

- Education for the environment involves developing informed concern about, and encouraging sensitive use of, the environment now and in the future. The focus is on sustainable solutions to environmental problems, taking into account the fact that there are conflicting interests an different perspectives, and informing the choices that we all have to make. (SCAA, 1996)

Environmental education is seen not as a discrete subject in its own right, but as a cross-curricular theme, requiring contributions from a variety of subject areas. The Government stresses that it is up to schools to decide how to develop cross-curricular themes. In his report, Sir Ron Dearing (1994) explains that in addition to the time given to environmental education through the teaching of statutory subjects, 20 per cent of time on the timetable can be used at the discretion of individual schools. This offers additional opportunities for schools to develop this area of the curriculum and extend their work to include environmental planning projects.

Education for participation

Public participation in planning is not just a slogan from the 1960s, it is written into our planning legislation. But it can only become a reality if we rear a generation capable of coping with the issues involved. In our slow and faltering evolution into a genuinely participatory democracy, this is the challenge to be taken up by the teacher involved in environmental education. (Ward, 1995)

Through provision in a number of subject areas, particularly geography and design and technology, as well as in cross-curricular themes of environmental education, citizenship, personal and social education, moral education and economic awareness, studies in schools can promote education for participation. Education for participation is not new. The publication of the Skeffington Report in 1969 heralded an explosion of initiatives in the 1970s to develop an education based on social justice principles, to create a more active and involved citizenry. Since then, many schools have tackled environmental design projects, focusing on how the environment is shaped and controlled, involving pupils between the ages of five and 18 in planning projects.

Design education

The planning and development process is about shaping and controlling the environment. It is about anticipating and dealing with the experience of change. Change is the only certainty we have: whether slow and imperceptible or sudden and dramatic, even traumatic, it is the only thing we know will happen. How can young people be helped to deal with change positively, creatively and responsibly? How can they develop the skills and capabilities to participate effectively in a democratic society to ensure that we take appropriate action in relation to the environment and use resources responsibly? How can they adapt to changing circumstances and know how to create a sustainable future for themselves and others? The design process is about thinking ahead, anticipating, making plans, considering alternative possibilities and thinking how things might be. It is about visualizing the future and making it happen.

Design education is a challenging area of work for schools. Although it is

LIVERPOOL
JOHN MOORES UNIVERSITY
AVRIL ROBARTS LRC
TEL. 0151 231 4022

generally seen as within the province of design and technology, environmental design studies also include aspects of art and geography. The emphasis must be on developing young people's capacities to conceptualise, devise and create. It requires speculative thinking, developing the skills for hypothesis, supposition and imaginative projection, where pupils are able to consider alternatives or future possibilities. Imagination is used to confront and create reality. Invention and innovation are the results of creative thinking. Fancy and fantasy have a place, not as an escape but as a means of coming to grips with the world, of making it and creating it anew. Ken Baynes summarises the nature of design in education :

Design is essentially speculative and propositional. It is about the future. All its methods and procedures are directed towards deciding how places, products and images will be. In this respect, it is highly unusual in a curriculum dealing primarily with the past and what we already know. Design is not only knowing about the future, it is about imagining it, shaping it and bringing it about. This needs to be emphasised and made real in learning. (Baynes, 1982)

Environmental design education involves experience of architecture, planning, landscape, urban design, building and interior design. Although this whole area is much influenced by technology, social need and economics, it is also crucially about the visual and formal qualities of places and buildings. Without this perception, the environment comes to represent only utilitarian values and to neglect the aesthetic, the social and the spiritual.

Education for citizenship

The National Curriculum requires schools to address citizenship, economic awareness and personal and social education. In addition, schools are expected to deal with moral education. All these subjects can potentially contribute to education for participation. Connections between environmental education and citizenship were identified at a conference organised jointly by the Department for Education and the Department of the Environment (1995). The prospectus explained: 'Schools can help pupils to develop the knowledge, understanding and skills they need to make informed judgements and in later life to make a valued contribution to decisions, whether in their own immediate locality or more widely'.

The Right Honourable Gillian Shephard, MP, then Secretary of State for Education and Employment, held the view that: 'as citizens of tomorrow, the pupils of today will be called on to help frame national decisions about the allocation of resources which will have profound consequences for the environment' (Department for Education and Department of the Environment, 1995). There is an important connection between education for citizenship and effective participation in environmental planning. According to the National Curriculum Council (1990a), areas of study included in citizenship are:

- the nature of the community

- roles and relationships in a pluralist society

- duties, responsibilities and rights of being a citizen

- the family

- democracy in action

- the citizen and the law

- work, employment and leisure

- public services

There is further government support for citizenship to be found in both the Citizen's Charter (1991) and the Parents' Charter (1991): 'The Citizen's Charter is about giving more power to the citizen. But citizenship is about our responsibilities – as parents, for example, or as neighbours – as well as our entitlements; the Citizen's Charter is not a recipe for more state action; it is a testament of our belief in people's right to be informed and choose for themselves' (Taylor, 1992).

To be effective, education for citizenship needs to develop beyond the boundaries of formal education in schools to involve the voluntary sector and other agencies as well as members of the community. This is echoed in a report (Uzzell, 1994) which is critical of treating environmental education as a formal area of study in schools, and recommends the development of a more proactive and participatory citizenry. It advocates a review of established approaches:

> Environmental education is more than just about raising levels of awareness and changing attitudes and behaviours. Environmental education has to be seen in a larger context ... of action competence ... It requires a positive approach to cooperative decision-making, a respect for democracy and an understanding of participatory processes .... The school will have to open itself in new ways to families and the local community, it will have to come to be seen as an active agent in the creation of change rather than a passive transmitter of information or values. (Uzzell, 1994)

Youth service

Environmental education is not just a concern for schools, but the responsibility of a number of community agencies. The British Government Panel on Sustainable Development (1996) recommends that 'the Government should develop a comprehensive strategy for environmental education and training to cover both formal and informal education and to bring in the wide range of related activities by official and voluntary bodies, industry and commerce, and local communities'.

Education for participation is echoed in the approach of the youth service, which sees the need for young people to be able to develop capacities, accept responsibilities and evaluate the contexts in which they live and act accordingly (*Effective Youth Worker*, 1991). The principles which form the basis of the National Curriculum in schools provide a focus for youth work:

- breadth (of learning and experience)

- balance (through interaction over shorter and longer periods)

- relevance (to suit the young person's interest, experience and aptitudes)

- differentiation (through styles and contexts rather than an imbalance of learning experience)

- progression and continuity (flexible rather than prescribed)

Three key reports informed the development of the youth work curriculum. The Albemarle Report (1960) focused on young people's personal development and emphasised the idea of social education through leisure. The Milson–Fairbairn Report (1969) stressed the need for the social and political integration of young people and saw youth work as providing and promoting education and experience for membership of the 'active society'. Great emphasis was placed on the participation of young people, and the concept of political education was introduced as an area in which the youth service should be involved. The Thompson Report, *Experience and Participation* (1982), 'challenged the youth service to generate greater participation by young people, stressed the need to foster and improve the links which existed between the voluntary and statutory sectors and also to create effective management structures and processes'.

Concern for equal opportunities has dominated the implementation of the youth work curriculum, creating a backcloth against which young people's active participation in environmental planning can flourish. A series of three ministerial conferences in 1989, 1990 and 1991 established a basis for the development of youth work. The first generated the 'Statement of Purpose', which explained the purpose of youth work as:

> seeking to redress all forms of inequality and to ensure equality of opportunity for all young people to fulfil their potential as empowered individuals and members of groups and communities and to support young people during transition to adulthood. Youth work should, therefore, offer opportunities which are educative, designed to promote equality of opportunity, facilitate participation and seek to empower young people. (Albemarle Report, 1960)

A key element in youth work is experiential learning. This is part of the 'progressive' curriculum, where, through reflection upon and making sense of previous experience, what is learnt is invested in new experience, enabling young people to take responsibility for their own development. The two main approaches are, firstly, developing concern and encouraging debate about environmental issues and, secondly, direct action. Most young people are aware of the slogan 'think globally, act locally' and are keen to adopt the imperative of local action. Many young people are contributing to adults' efforts to consider the qualities they value in their neighbourhood and are helping to shape the plans and prepare programmes for local action to improve the quality of their lives and their environment.

At a conference on 'Young People and the Environment' (Council for Environmental Education, 1996a), the main issue under discussion was how to secure young people's ideas and energies and engage their participation in environmental action. The general assumption was that young people were both idealistic and practical and, through direct action, wanted both to protect the environment and to contribute more positively to improve the quality of life. Tom Wylie, chief executive of the National Youth Agency, identified profound changes in society's value system, which had led to a greater emphasis on the individual and which stressed competitiveness rather than promoting concern for the group, society or the common good. Only those things which could be quantified seemed to be valued, he argued. Now was the time to re-assert different values, such as human solidarity. Tom Wylie feared that the involvement of young people in environmental issues and environmental action was in danger of being fragmented and short term. He thought there might be a danger of young people being too willing to do things before thinking too much about the implications of their actions or their possible impact upon the environment. This indicates two other key elements in the relationship between awareness and action. There is a need to develop a critical stance to weigh up the pros and cons of a situation, so that people understand the nature of the value judgements which inform action. It is also necessary to engage in environmental design or planning activities to create opportunities to consult others, generate ideas for change and test them out before putting them into practice.

National organisations

Support for environmental education has come not only from the formal education sector and the youth service, but also from a number of national organisations and professional associations. They offer support in a variety of ways: by carrying out research and development projects, producing publications, organising professional development and training programmes, promoting campaigns, award schemes and competitions.

A key influence has been the *Bulletin of Environmental Education (BEE)*, published in the 1970s and 1980s by the Town and Country Planning Association, then subsequently, *Streetwise*, published by the National Association for Urban Studies. This has promoted the participation of young people in the planning and decision-making processes. In the 1970s and 1980s, a national network of urban studies centres and architecture workshops brought environment, design and education professionals together to work with young people. Sadly, these centres are rapidly disappearing because of problems of core funding. However, the new millennium and the prospect of significant change might stimulate a reappraisal of the value of such a valuable resource to engage people in the process of change. It remains to be seen whether the newly created architecture centres, which will need to rely heavily on sponsorship for their education programmes, will be able to take over where urban studies centres and architecture workshops left off.

The Council for Environmental Education (CEE) is an umbrella organisation for environmental and education organisations, some of which advocate education for participation. A recent CEE initiative has been to establish a Built Environment Education group of organisations concerned with heritage, design and cultural interests to focus on the challenge of the urban environment. The aim is to create more positive perceptions of the built environment, establish a stronger lobby for built environment education and create an impetus for research and development. In 1996, CEE secured funding for three years from the Department for Education and Employment to develop, in association with other environmental agencies, a National Young People's Environment Network (NYPEN) aimed primarily at 13- to 19-year-olds, which will act as a stimulus for raising awareness of environmental issues and, hopefully, lead to action for environmental improvement (CEE, 1996b).

Influenced by government commitment to Local Agenda 21, the intention is that environmental youth work will empower young people to make changes to develop a more sustainable way of living. The network will provide opportunities for consultation through local, regional and national forums such as the children's conference, 'Leave it to Us', held in Eastbourne in 1995 and the Roundtable for young people held at Camden in 1996. Through the development of regional groups, the hope is to establish a national environmental youth movement to address young people's concerns related to the environment and enable them to do something about them. A pilot project was set up in Bath in 1997, and the programme will be expanded to form six regional groups. Each project will have financial support for travel and programme costs and funding for a regional facilitator.

The World Wide Fund for Nature (WWF UK) has an extensive education programme and a wide range of publications aimed at developing in young people an increased understanding of environmental issues and promoting change in attitudes and behaviours in relation to lifestyles. It has developed an in-service programme for teachers, 'Reaching Out', which seeks to involve teachers and their pupils in education for sustainability. This implies not only a more responsible use of diminishing resources, but a greater involvement in decision-making and greater responsibility for environmental management.

The Tidy Britain Group has worked for years to encourage young people to care for their environment. The Eco-Schools Award Scheme is promoted by the 'Going for Green' campaign, funded by the Government, and managed by the Tidy Britain Group. Among its aims are to increase environmental awareness, improve the school environment and involve the local community. Schools are helped to establish a framework for developing a programme of environmental education and for improving their systems of managing resources and caring for their environment. It encourages the involvement of children in decision-making and action.

Other environmental agencies such as wildlife trusts are lending further support. For example, the Royal Society for the Protection of Birds (RSPB) is extending its work to encompass a wider view of environmental education. Its recent publication in collaboration with the CEE, *Our World, Our Responsibility* (RSPB/CEE, 1995), has promoted a campaign for schools to develop a cross-curricular policy for environmental education.

The Countryside Commission, English Nature and English Heritage have worked to encourage young people to become involved in Agenda 21 initiatives and have promoted the development of various kinds of groups to facilitate their involvement in developing sustainable lifestyles. These have required the development of interpersonal skills of group working, negotiation and joint decision-making. The aim is to support people involved in caring for and improving their local environment through practical projects and management schemes.

Agencies such as the British Trust for Conservation Volunteers create opportunities for young people to engage in projects which offer them experience of actually changing the environment. Nature conservation schemes, tree planting, canal clearing and pond making are all projects which young people have joined in enthusiastically.

Some commercial organisations have developed environmental education initiatives such as the Shell 'Better Britain' campaign, which is a partnership of 15 organisations with Shell UK, providing information, grants and advice to local groups. Indeed, many agencies, both governmental and nongovernmental, choose campaigns, award schemes and competitions as a mechanism for making contacts with individuals, schools, community groups and other organisations to promote environmental awareness and encourage participation in environmental action.

The efforts of organisations to promote young people's participation in environmental planning are usually well publicised and high profile, endorsed by media personalities who adopt the role of environmentalists. Although the amount of money which is made available to participants in terms of awards and prizes is comparatively small, through extensive publicity and widespread dissemination of their ideas, these organisations create a set of expectations and practices which will benefit a greater number, not just those who win. On the other hand, organisations obtain a lot of publicity for comparatively little investment, particularly through the wonderful photo opportunities provided by happy children involved in environmental activities. There are also social justice issues raised by the use of competitions, which inevitably create more losers than winners, though perhaps it can be argued that it is not the winning, but the taking part that counts. Similarly, award schemes can provide public acknowledgement of effort and good practice for only a handful of participants, but many more might benefit from having been involved. A particular problem with one-off projects, competitions and awards is that they might have the appearance of creating opportunities for participation, but their educational value may be limited, with an emphasis on performance and immediate solutions rather than long-term development.

However, there is benefit in high-profile widespread publicity. Some organisations arrange media events to develop young people's awareness of environmental issues and engage them in environmental action. The Civic Trust has designated a week as 'Environment Week' and Learning through Landscapes has worked to establish 'School Grounds Day' in an effort to create high-profile activities which focus attention on the efforts of those involved in environmental education and to celebrate young people's achievements. The two examples which follow illustrate national organisations' attempts to link children's involvement in both planning and action, resulting in environmental improvement. The work of Groundwork Trust often takes place in neighbourhood settings, while Learning through Landscapes focuses on the school environment.

Groundwork Trust

The aim of Groundwork Trust is to work in partnership with all sections of the community – people, business and organisations – to help them safeguard and improve their environment and to create a better place in which to live and work. It reports that it has developed initiatives in 120 towns and cities, including 4000 regeneration projects, involving 46,000 volunteers and over 117,000 school children. Projects have included derelict land reclamation, energy conservation, school–industry links, green audits for business and housing estate renewal. The work is based on two complementary objectives: the personal development of the young people themselves; and the creation, through their endeavours, of new community facilities from which all members of the community can benefit.

However, John Davidson, Groundwork Trust's chief executive, has voiced reservations:

> All too often young people can be provided with opportunities to get involved in a predetermined project: a day planting a community woodland, for instance, developing a nature area or creating new routeways ... Whilst this kind of involvement holds great value ... these occasions did not always give young people real opportunities to take many, or any, decisions for themselves. Carried too far, they could simply have become a volunteer labour force, with no chance to develop their own ideas.

This disquiet was echoed by Dilwyn Evans, of Groundwork Trust, Nottinghamshire, who warned against the danger of one-off projects. He reported that although tree-planting schemes were worthwhile, there was a danger that they might be carried out with no thought given to their aftercare or maintenance. Recognising that 60 per cent of the tree-planting schemes carried out by

Groundwork had suffered damage, he felt it was important for young people to devise their own projects and take ownership of them. The key concern, in his view, was to find ways of encouraging young people to play a more active role in volunteering, to help monitor environmental change and take some responsibility for the protection and maintenance of their surroundings (Council for Environmental Education, 1996a).

On a more optimistic note, a specific link between environmental action and environmental design has been established by a Groundwork project called Green IT. This is sponsored by Rio Tinto Zinc, the mining company. Groundwork explains that it is

> about young people in school using design packages on computers to work up ideas for environmental improvements to the exteriors of local companies. The young people discuss their ideas with the company's managers and present their final designs. They have to offer reasons why certain options have been chosen and how their suggestions affect the total cost of the scheme. Once convinced, the business then pays for the improvements to be made.

Learning through Landscapes

School grounds are an important focus for young people's participation in environmental change. In 1986, a research project, Learning through Landscapes, was set up to investigate how educational opportunity could be extended and how environmental quality could be improved in school grounds (Adams, 1990b). In 1990, the Learning through Landscapes Trust was established to address these issues. The development programme which it has put into effect has encouraged schools all over the country to consider how to develop their grounds as a precious educational resource and advise them on how to protect and enhance them. The Trust reports that in the six years of its existence it has helped more than 10,000 schools, possibly involving more than 2,000,000 young people, in an area of land covering more than 50,000 acres.

Young people's involvement in changing the environment of their school grounds is different from other contexts in which they may operate. Changing their own gardens, planning a tree-planting initiative in part of a local park or being part of a major planning exercise has quite different 'rules' from changing the grounds of a school. *Special Places: Special People* (Titman, 1994) suggests that the school has a particular meaning for young people. It is a significant environment for young people, being the first public environment in which children can feel themselves to be 'stakeholders'.

Through an extensive publications programme, a membership scheme, a national network of regional coordinators and a variety of training initiatives, the Learning through Landscapes Trust has supported the development of school grounds as an educational resource across the curriculum. A current focus is to create opportunities for education for participation. Teenagers, for instance, are increasingly using student councils as a forum for learning the skills for participation. This always involves partnership with adults. Young people's experience and ideas are valued in generating ideas for change, but it is adults who worry about health and safety issues, sign insurance policies and locate the funds to finance the work. In Chapter 11, reports of children's participation in school grounds developments show the ways in which they approach the challenge of developing the school environment.

Why?
Whether environmental education is promoted through the efforts of those in the formal system of schooling, in informal education within the youth service or through the work of national organisations, young people need to believe there is some point to it all. This is not the same as motivation. It is a deeper, underlying belief that sustains and nourishes their involvement, and promotes a sense of commitment (Postman, 1996). Postman offers the idea of 'narratives' that give point to education. Among others, he identifies 'spaceship earth' which evokes a sense of responsibility to the planet, and the 'fallen angel' which reveals that we are all capable of making mistakes but that we can correct them. These messages underlie much of what is being promoted through environmental education and environmental action. Young people's participation in environmental planning gives tangible expression to their hope of a better future.

CHAPTER 4   Education for participation

This chapter explores the nature of participation in relation to young people's involvement in environmental planning and raises issues concerning its operation and effectiveness.

What is participation?

One of the purposes of this book is to encourage the view that young people should have a role in the development of their communities and their environment. Participation involves consultation to clarify what young people's needs and aspirations are. It is about the questions that need to be asked before the technical details of how to make available the necessary resources are tackled. It throws up conflicts of interest and then involves negotiation and compromise. Participation requires young people to make decisions and act upon them. How can they be helped to understand the complex issues involved in environmental change and management? It is clear that the notion of young people's participation in planning requires a careful analysis of what this means for them and for the adults who support them. This will have implications for the ways in which we can create opportunities for participation and how we make the experience meaningful and worthwhile for the young people and the communities of which they are a part.

Why participate?

So often, the impetus for participation in planning comes about because people feel threatened or are fearful about environmental change. More positively, it may be motivated by a desire to be involved with community issues, to do something and perhaps reinforce a sense of belonging. In analysing the need to encourage young people's participation, Play-Train, an independent training and development agency for play work, identifies the following (Play-Train, 1995):

• the child's right to be consulted and to have their views taken into account

• the need to understand the child's wants and needs

- the need to make provision more responsive to users
- the need to address developmental issues
- the need for social and political education
- the need to see children as creators not consumers
- the need for children to participate in a wider society
- the need for democracy

These themes are taken up in other arenas. For instance, the UK Strategy for Sustainable Development recommends consultation with young people about environmental issues, improving their understanding of the relationship between human activities, the environment and the concept of sustainable development, and providing a context within the National Curriculum for pupils to examine environmental issues.

However, young people's participation in environmental planning will not necessarily happen because the need is there, or it is thought to be a good thing, or because of increased opportunity. It will happen through education – not by the young learning about it, but by doing it.

Participation is an essential part of environmental education and by encouraging pupils to become involved in both the planning and implementation of initiatives related to their own environment they will become active contributors to society rather than spectators or critics. Experience has shown that where such participation takes place, local people are more likely to take an interest in and care for their environment (RSPB/CEE, 1995).

Frameworks for participation

It is clear that education for participation does not happen only within the school and that people other than teachers need to make a positive contribution. To be effective, education for participation needs involvement by the community and with the community. For young people, this may involve a working contact with a wide range of adults, including those from the professional, business and commercial sectors, as well as local residents and voluntary organisations. These may be stimulated by school projects or youth work initiatives. It is important that young people encounter a range of attitudes and opinions which are not necessarily mediated by the teacher or youth worker.

Robert Cowan, a planner with a long interest in participation, suggests that another way of looking at the notion of 'participation' is to replace it with that of 'collaboration', where there is a much clearer understanding of the different roles people can have in the development process and a more egalitarian view of the relationships between them (Cowan, 1995). His view is that people can only play an effective part in a project if they have equal access to the seven requirements of collaboration:

- information

- contacts with networks

- knowledge of their relationship to the city-wide context

- inspiration from experience elsewhere

- access to skills and professionals

- opportunity to collaborate with other people and organisations

- a role in the formal planning processes through which planning decisions are made

There are many ways in which people can participate and there are many degrees of participation. In 1969, Sherry Arnstein, referring to adult involvement in planning in the USA, described a 'ladder of participation', which ranged from non-participation through tokenism to degrees of empowerment. The lowest level was manipulation, then it ranged through therapy, informing, consultation, placation, partnership, delegated power, to citizen control at the highest level. David Wilcox adapted Arnstein's framework and offered advice on how to participate, identifying five areas as important: information, consultation, deciding together, acting together and supporting independent community interests (Wilcox, 1994).

Is it participation?

Roger Hart (1992) saw participation as generally referring 'to the process of sharing decisions which affect one's life and the life of the community in which one lives'. He reworked Arnstein's ladder of participation to suggest the following levels (Hart, 1997a) (see Figure 2):

- *Manipulation* – This is where children do not understand the issues involved and hence do not understand their actions. They just go along with what adults require of them.

- *Decoration* – This is where children wear T-shirts with slogans, perform at an event to bolster a cause, or are used as photo opportunities to provide smiling faces and engage in fun activities to create a 'feel-good' factor. They probably enjoy it and participate in the event with enthusiasm, but they will have little idea what it is about and have no say in its organisation.

- *Tokenism* – Often, well-meaning adults organise situations where children are apparently given a voice, but have little choice about the subject and limited opportunity to formulate their own opinions. This occurs when adults set the agenda and children are expected to perform appropriately. The degree to which the experience is shaped and controlled by adults will determine the level of tokenism involved.

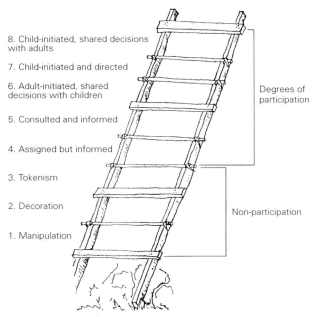

8. Child-initiated, shared decisions with adults

7. Child-initiated and directed

6. Adult-initiated, shared decisions with children

5. Consulted and informed

4. Assigned but informed

3. Tokenism

2. Decoration

1. Manipulation

Degrees of participation

Non-participation

Figure 2 The ladder of participation, showing eight levels of young people's participation in projects. (The ladder metaphor is borrowed from an essay on adult participation by Sherry Arnstein (1969); the categories are new.) Reproduced with permission from Hart, R A (1997a) *Children's Participation: The Theory and Practice of Involving Young Citizens in Community Development and Environmental Care*. UNICEF, New York, and Earthscan, London.

- *Assigned but informed* – Here adults formulate the framework and processes for participation, and children participate voluntarily when they have understood the intentions of the project, know who made decisions concerning their involvement and appreciate the nature of their role.

- *Consulted and informed* – The project may be designed and run by adults, but children understand the process and their opinions are treated seriously. Children are not expected to reflect adult perceptions and opinions, but are encouraged to develop their own ideas and understandings and helped to make informed judgements.

- *Adult-initiated, shared decisions with children* – The goal here is to involve everyone in formulating ideas and planning projects. The experience and particular knowledge of both children and adults are valued and they are able to find ways of communicating with each other. This is where adults are willing to hand over control of the ideas to the children, while providing a secure framework and perhaps some direction.

- *Child-initiated and directed* – This is where children take the lead in organising and directing collaborative working groups, supported by adults. Here, children have been able to develop the confidence and competence to take control and responsibility.

- *Child-initiated, shared decisions with adults* – Children take a lead role in conceptualising ideas and proposals, identifying opportunities and problems and formulating strategies for action, the process supported by adults.

Is the metaphor of the ladder a useful one in environmental education? Children faced with ladders of success and achievement might not welcome yet another ladder to climb. It perhaps suggests a hierarchy or step-by-step sequence. However, for young people to develop the necessary capabilities and understandings, all the levels of participation have some value. Not all projects and opportunities will permit the same kind or same degree of involvement. Children cannot suddenly be involved in ways which demand high levels of skill, without having had other opportunities to gain experience and develop some measure of confidence and competence. Therefore what is learned from one experience may be reinvested in subsequent involvement. The effect is cumulative and long term. It may result in young people developing a capability for involvement but, in Hart's view, 'empowerment' may not be an appropriate goal:

> I don't use the word 'empowerment'. This is because I associate it with other important, but very different movements for the rights of oppressed groups and for women's rights. Children are different in that they are developing individuals within all of these groups. Child rights advocates sometimes reduce the complexity of human development to a simplistic call for children to have power with a voice equal to adults in decision-making. This is patently silly, for children's ability to participate in all this develops gradually. (Hart, 1997b)

Consultation or participation?

There is sometimes confusion about the difference between 'consultation' and 'participation'. The difference is apparent when children are consulted, perhaps through questionnaires, but given no feedback or explanation of how their views have contributed to increased understanding or have led to particular action. It is also evident when adults ask children for their ideas for environmental change and are delighted to receive drawings, maps and plans. These are then reworked by adults to create a kind of composite design. Sometimes it is claimed that this is the children's design, but individual children do not recognise it as theirs. Or it is claimed as the work of the designer, whose synthesis of children's ideas has been miraculously transformed into an original work. What is missing in both cases is the children's involvement in a real experience of design, which exposes them to conflicting values, real constraints, limits on choices and difficult decisions, a process which possibly ends in compromise.

Barriers to participation

There are constraints and inhibitions which work against the notion of young people's participation in environmental change and design activities. A key influence is people's attitudes. Some adults perceive young people as a problem rather than a source of ideas and enthusiasm. Some organisations have involved young people in the development of schemes for environmental change with great success. Others have been more diffident and, whilst recognising that ideally children should be consulted, have not chosen to involve them to any great extent. Others thought that it would not benefit their work to consult young people. Some have been overwhelmed by the potential obstacles or have simply considered it an inappropriate thing to do.

It is not always easy to facilitate young people's participation. Adults tend to dominate in creating the framework for participation, determining the extent of young people's involvement and setting the agenda for discussion or action. If they are included, young people are confined to the periphery. Not all local authorities are excited at the prospect of participation, especially by young people, possibly because it may affect the established roles of professional officers and elected members:

> citizen participation is presented as modern-day democracy while the underlying
> intention is to impose authoritarian structures in the neighbourhoods involved ... the
> tendency is for elected members to perceive resident participation as a threat to their
> own position ... and for officers to consider that the function of residents' groups

should be to support, not criticize their role ... authority's tendency when confronted with grassroots pressures for change is to diffuse, dilute and redirect the energies originally directed towards change. (McArthur, 1995)

It is not possible for young people to be representative of well-defined constituencies in decision-making processes because they are not a homogeneous group. Each young person will have particular concerns and perspectives, and individuals do not necessarily represent the views of a group. Problems for both adult citizens and young people alike are the complexity of the planning process, and the formal structures and bureaucratic procedures within which decisions are made. It may be difficult for them to understand the technical language which is used. Community participants do not have the same status as professional officers or elected members. Not all decision-making procedures are clear and easy to grasp, and some may be out of sight of the democratic process. Developing policy and agreeing strategy is a lengthy business, involving debate, argument, bargaining, deals, disappointments and compromise and it is sometimes difficult for young people to sustain an involvement when nothing seems to be happening. Also, many young people feel that they have little control over their lives, so they cannot conceive that they might have any influence on what the environment could be like. They do not see themselves as taking a proactive stance or see a role for themselves in shaping the environment in the future. They view this as the province of adults.

Many young people become disillusioned as they discover that awareness and concern do not appear to lead to action or change. Also many young people have never seen a role for themselves within their own environment and cannot imagine their surroundings and lives as things which can be changed through their own actions. It is vital to address these issues by offering opportunities for real and meaningful participation (McArthur, 1995).

At a Roundtable organised by the Local Government Management Board (1996), it was evident that the following factors inhibit young people's involvement:

- disillusion with the process – too much talk and too little action

- disillusion with those in power

- irrelevance to young people's lives or priorities

- they sense hostility and lack of interest, or feel they are not taken seriously

- lack of access to information

- lack of understanding of the way the system works

- peer pressure

- lack of money and time to get involved

A similar list is suggested by Play-Train, who see young people's attitudes as crucial in determining their preparedness to participate. They identify preconceived attitudes, old habits, laziness, jargon, time and pressure, short-termism, parent power, fear, lack of training and lack of vision as barriers to young people's involvement (Play-Train, 1995). There are also factors which inhibit institutions from encouraging young people to participate: there may be no clear policy; policies may be in place, but no effective strategies have been developed; resources may be diverted into other initiatives; it may be nobody's particular responsibility.

Benefits of participation

There is a greater likelihood that through direct involvement, young people will develop an interest in environmental issues, a concern for environmental improvement and the motivation to play an active part in shaping their environment in the future. In many instances, children's ideas and proposals have extended and enriched adult thinking about environmental change and have acted as catalysts for adult involvement. Where children have been involved in school grounds and playground developments, they have encouraged their parents and neighbours to contribute to environmental change. Professionals who have been involved in working with young people in this context have found the experience satisfying and worthwhile and it has often given them insights and techniques which can be used when working with adults.

Where young people have learnt techniques and skills of participation, these can be transferred to other situations and contribute to community development. Where they have been involved in formulating and developing ideas for change, the experience has influenced their perceptions of the environment and the meaning it has for them: they are more likely to view it positively and have a stronger attachment to it. Their concern is more likely to be turned into positive engagement in the process of change, rather than raising objections to it. There is a big difference between feeling a sense of involvement and responsibility for creating changes and having change determined by others and thrust upon you.

Chris Church, coordinator of the 'Percentage for Participation' campaign, explains that effective participation can add value for society – through less dissatisfaction, vandalism, etc. – and reduce the time and costs of planning appeals etc. by dealing with problems at an early stage. Research carried out for the Department of the Environment in 1994 suggests that 'at its best, community involvement can enable processes to be speeded up, resources to be used more effectively, product quality and feelings of local ownership to improve, added value to emerge, confidence and skills increase for all and conflicts to be more readily resolved'. (Church, 1996)

Through projects such as those described in the case studies in Part II, young people learn a range of skills and techniques for participation which enable them to contribute ideas for enhancing the quality of their environment. They develop critical skills as well as communication and social skills, and begin to experience some of the essential features of participation – team working, negotiation, visualising change and conflict resolution. They gain new insights and deeper understanding and appreciation of places where they live, work and play. They are able to clarify their own values as well as those of others. They are able to think about ideas and strategies for change and improvement. All of these experiences are important and represent skills and learning which are transferable and which can form the basis of an active participation in environmental matters as adults.

PARTICIPATION IN PRACTICE

Figure 3 Younger and older members of a community meet planners to discuss the design of a proposed housing development in Newcastle

Part II provides detailed accounts of 20 initiatives and projects where young people have been involved in making proposals for change. It explains how the projects arose, how young people and adults worked to develop their ideas, and comments on the outcomes.

The reports demonstrate young people's interest in and concern for the environment, and explain their efforts to improve environmental quality. They look to the future and feel positively about change. In all the projects, they have been supported by adults to help them understand the issues involved and develop appropriate strategies to deal with the tasks they set themselves.

CHAPTER 5 Introduction to the case studies

This chapter provides a brief overview of the case studies, describing the different types of approach used and the various levels of participation. It also discusses the reasons for selecting the particular examples included in the book.

Against the background of national policy and the efforts of organisations described in Part I, perhaps in the face of institutional lethargy, individuals and groups have worked to create opportunities for children and young people to participate in planning for environmental change. The case studies described in Part II provide examples of young people's efforts to change attitudes and behaviours towards the environment, formulate proposals for change and in some cases, implement their ideas. Three different, yet related, approaches are evident. Firstly, there have been opportunities to discuss and debate environmental issues. Secondly, there have been opportunities to engage in planning activities, conceptualising ideas for change, and proposing alternatives for the way we shape and control our environment. Thirdly, there has been direct action upon the environment in clean-up schemes, tree-planting projects and initiatives to raise awareness to encourage a more responsible use of resources. In some cases, through encouraging debate, engaging young people in the experience of planning and environmental design and perhaps putting their ideas into practice, there has been an attempt to link environmental awareness and environmental action.

The selection of examples
Children and young people have worked with adults in a variety of contexts. The choice of examples reveals a geographical spread of initiatives in urban and suburban locations, in both formal and informal educational settings in England, Scotland and Wales. Those included here are only a glimpse of the hundreds of projects which have taken place over the last few years. The examples are not representative of all the different approaches evident in

current initiatives, but they do suggest the kinds of projects which are possible. They have been selected to show different facets of a complex picture. It has been possible to identify similarities and differences in the ideas, emphases, working methods and outcomes of the various ways of working. The following categories which reflect different opportunities for participation by children and young people, have been chosen for ease of reference:

* Local Agenda 21 groups and youth forums (Chapter 6)

* research (Chapter 7)

* local plans and urban development plans (Chapter 8)

* urban regeneration (Chapter 9)

* art, design and environment (Chapter 10)

* school grounds (Chapter 11)

The choice of case studies demonstrates differing degrees of participation and examples illuminate different aspects of the process. Some emphasise the children's ideas, others the methods of engagement, others the impact on the environment or the impact on the participants. They describe the nature of the projects, the roles and relationships of the people involved and how they worked together. They also reveal young people's concerns about the environment and provide a glimpse of their hopes for change. In many cases, mention is made of the knowledge, understanding, skills and capabilities they developed through the experience. Projects have involved children and young people from three to 18 years old. There has been no attempt to highlight differences in gender, ethnicity or ability; young people have not been labelled as disadvantaged or disabled. The idea is that all children and young people have the capacity to participate. Their ability to do so will depend on experience, learning, opportunity and the support of sympathetic and interested adults.

Approaches

The case studies reveal a wide range of opportunities for young people to participate in planning, environmental design and environmental change. They illuminate interactions between participants and report on the variety of working relations between adults and young people. Two very different strands emerge. Although complementary, one is primarily concerned with the *consultation* process, and the other with the *design* process. The case studies reveal that through the work of youth groups and forums and involvement in adult research projects, children and young people have been able to discuss environmental issues and make their views known. Others involved in urban regeneration, art and design and school grounds initiatives have been able to do this through the medium of environmental design projects. In some cases they have been able to realise their ideas.

Levels of participation

The varied approaches to the management of projects reflect the different levels of participation. The stimulus and context for participation will influence the nature of young people's involvement. In some cases, the efforts may only result in a number of complaints together with a 'wish list' of amenities or facilities which they would like to see. It may result in a vision of a better environment and a plan for action. Sometimes it is possible for young people to engage in a sustained design exercise where the current situation is carefully analysed and evaluated before different options for change are considered and their impact on the environment anticipated. In some cases, it has been possible for young people to create opportunities to monitor and evaluate the impact of their proposals and perhaps take some responsibility for care and maintenance.

CHAPTER 6   Local Agenda 21 groups, youth forums

Local Agenda 21 has made the environment a focus for the work of many youth groups. They meet to discuss environmental issues, consider what might be done for environmental protection and in many cases organise action for environmental improvement. Local and regional forums and national conferences create opportunities for discussion and debate.

The case studies in this chapter reveal the thinking which underpins the development of youth groups. Young people have found ways to organise themselves to carry out investigations, to organise meetings and plan programmes. They have debated environmental problems and presented proposals for change to their local council through collaborating with planners or at meetings with elected members. They have addressed themselves to the school community, consulting other pupils, teachers, governors, parents and neighbours about their ideas for development. They have created programmes and campaigns to raise other people's awareness of environmental issues, to influence attitudes to the environment and, hopefully, change people's behaviour.

It takes a lot of energy to set up the framework for young people's forums, and organisers need to be satisfied that they are creating opportunities for an appropriate level of participation. However, it is all too easy to identify problems without being able to formulate strategies to deal with them: discussions may result in worthy resolutions but not generate any action. They might even succeed in shifting responsibility for action onto other people – there is a tendency to agree that 'they' should do something about the problem under consideration. There may also be the possibility of tokenism, where the 'feel-good' factor for organisers and participants overrides other considerations: 'the voice of young people is being heard', they think, simply through publicity.

Where groups are action oriented, there may be a danger that young people will be too willing to take action before thinking through the implications of their actions or their possible impact upon the environment. There is also a danger in the single-issue approach which does not recognise the complexity of dealing with change. On the other hand, by acting on a specific issue, young people will develop skills in dealing with change, which is an important aspect of social and political education. They might make contact with a range of people offering different perspectives on issues, which in turn helps them both clarify their own values as well as others'. In addition, they may develop a greater understanding of the planning system and gain insight into bureaucratic systems, the working of committees, how to achieve consensus and resolve conflict. They may also develop skills in lobbying and campaigning.

| CASE STUDY 1 | **Leeds** | |
| | **Setting up a Youth Forum** | Age 7–18+ |

This case study reports on the efforts of a local authority to establish a framework for a youth forum through an extensive consultation programme with young people. The report is based primarily on Ruse (1997).

Feasibility study

Since the development of a 'green strategy' in Leeds and its subsequent designation as 'Environment City', there has been a long-standing commitment by the City Council to the formation of an environmental youth forum as a method of enabling participation of children and young people in environmental planning within the city. Early in 1995, it commissioned the first phase of a feasibility study into the idea of a city-wide environmental youth group. The report considered the possibility of setting up a youth forum which would contribute the fourth arm of the Environment City Partnership, together with Leeds City Council, the business sector and the voluntary and community sector. Through a postal survey, youth workers and young people were asked their opinion of the idea. Most youth workers believed a forum would be an asset, as long as it did not create extra work for them. Young people were confused about what 'forum' meant. Most of them wanted practical environmental activities.

Further research

A second phase of research was set up to explore young people's reactions to the idea of a youth forum, to consider what form it might take and identify what funding would be required. A consultant was engaged by Leeds City Council to make contact with a cross-section of children and young people in a variety of settings. These were formal, such as schools and scout groups; semi-formal, such as youth clubs; and informal, such as street groups known to detached youth workers. Youth workers, young people and children were consulted as to what age range and format would be appropriate. A range of options for recording information was offered to children and young people, as was the option to participate. The most popular way of responding was through questionnaires facilitated by the researcher, youth workers or the young people themselves. The survey sample was 426 children and young people between the ages of seven and 21 years; 396 responses were received.

In considering the nature of the forum, the issues were:

- How might a forum be set up?

- How would a cross-section of children and young people be represented?

- What decision-making processes would be used?

- What 'style' would the forum adopt to suit the attitudes of the young people involved?

- How would the forum relate to a variety of needs – for instance, those perceived as being outside the mainstream 'cultures' of children: children with disabilities; children in care; children who are carers; young people who are 'unclubbable'?

Options

One suggestion was that the forum could be set up like a committee of the local authority, similar to a municipal children's council. Members of the forum would be directly elected from recognised bodies such as schools and youth clubs. Another possibility would be to set up a federal arrangement, where members would meet on the basis of a shared neighbourhood or common interest and elect one or more representatives to meet as a loose federation. Recommendations could go from this body to the local authority and other organisations. A third, less structured model could take the form of open assemblies covering clusters of neighbourhoods across the city. Each one could feed their views directly to city-wide organisations. Other possibilities for a forum might include a green drop-in centre with Internet facilities, connected with schools, youth clubs and libraries. A forum could also act as a useful networking tool to facilitate communication between projects and encourage environmental activity. This would require an effective means of communication.

Conclusions

The results of the consultation showed that environment ranked alongside crime, safety and vandalism as a priority concern for young people. The main themes emerging from the research were the importance of the local neighbourhood and peer links, as well as the difficulty children and young people have in relating to global environmental issues, particularly in terms of taking appropriate action. A preference for practical activities was expressed, confirming the findings of phase one of the feasibility study. Furthermore, although children and young people felt that they could make a contribution, they did not believe that anyone would listen to them. While some young people felt confident enough to articulate their views and opinions in a forum on environmental issues, this method would exclude the majority of young people whose priorities and interest either lay elsewhere or who lacked confidence to participate in that way.

To establish a forum, one solution might be to use the environmental organisations already working with children and young people in Leeds, to set up a quarterly 'talking shop'. However, such an initiative would include the more eloquent young people and those already active in environmental matters. It is doubtful whether setting up a forum with a city-wide remit on a single topic such as 'environment' would succeed. Given that the aim is to involve as wide a cross-section as possible, and also to engage those young people usually marginalised in such initiatives, a more appropriate mechanism needs to be developed which takes account of their needs and interests. It was also evident that any progress towards involving a wide range of children and young people in environmental issues could be made only if those issues were set in the context of people's own environment. A different definition of 'environment' has to be communicated to some young people, related to their own experience of the world and located firmly in the local environment.

CASE STUDY 2	**Brighton**	
	VOYCE	Age 11–18+

This case study reports on the work of a youth group concerned with environmental issues and engaged in a variety of campaigns for improving environmental quality. Their efforts are inspired by Agenda 21 and supported by the local authority.

The Brighton and Hove Community Environment Partnership (BriHCEP) is developing the Local Agenda 21 plan for the town. It is a four-way partnership of community and voluntary organisations, the business sector, environmental organisations and the public sector. It is 'committed to protecting and improving the local environment and quality of life in Brighton and Hove and to be as representative as possible of the many communities in the area'. It has joined the Regeneration Partnership to ensure that sustainability is an influential thread in the town's regeneration strategy and to bid for some of the money for sustainable development projects. BriHCEP takes action through a wide range of working groups, one of which is VOYCE (Views of Young Concerned Environmentalists), Brighton.

Organisation
An information leaflet produced by VOYCE explains that it was set up through Brighton and Hove Community Environment Partnership by a group of young people who are concerned with environmental protection and green issues. They meet once a month for an hour, or more frequently if activities demand it. Anyone between the ages of 11 and 25 can join. The group is supported by an officer in the Environmental Services Department at Brighton Borough Council. Early meetings focused on issues of membership and organisation of the group. A bank account was necessary so that monies raised from sponsorship could be deposited. Effective communication between group members was seen as important and a 'phone tree' set up to create a chain of messages. Other discussions focused on a logo for the group and on the content and presentation of an information leaflet. More ambitious ideas were for an information pack or booklet.

Activities
The group has focused primarily on Agenda 21 concerns:

- developing the group's understanding of environmental issues (guest speakers)

- environmental awareness initiatives and campaigns (can sculpture, cycle racks, Christmas tree recycling)

- environmental/pollution monitoring (survey of bus users, vehicle emissions, rescue mission indicators)

- environmental improvement schemes (litter collection, murals, recycled glass bricks, bottle clean-up, paper bank)

Interests
The following extracts from the minutes of the group's meetings indicate the

wide range of members' interests and the variety of activities in which they are involved:

- Any more environmental questionnaires? If so, please send them to Kim. Adam will collate the responses on computer so that we can produce a report for BriHCEP.

- Kim is selling mugs, £2.50 each. Money for World Wide Fund for Nature Project at Falmer School.

- Action Points – Magpie Mural cancelled due to bad weather. Re-schedule. Reschedule Dance Parade. VOYCE litter pick.

- Transport 2000 – Hannah will write a thank you letter. Possible group letter to buses or petition for change. Exhaust watch cards available from Kim to report cars/vans etc. causing pollution.

- Any more entries for the 'Visualising Vandalism' photo competition?

- Reporter from the *Brighton and Hove Leader* contacted me as he heard about our mural projects.

- Poor cycle lanes – need improvement due to cars parked and not continuous. Also sometimes no safer for cyclists and pedestrians on the beach.

But things do not always go smoothly. It was not easy to establish membership, create an effective system of communication and, as is the way for many adult groups, some members felt they had to shoulder too much of the burden. A note in the minutes of an early meeting reads:

No way of communicating with anyone. Lisa, Sarah and Kia feel it is unfair for them and the rest of the group that they organise everything. They want everyone to make decisions ... Kim apologised for involving them too much, but she needed to talk to people who knew what was going on and to make decisions etc. Sarah. Kia and Lisa say that it is unfair for them to make all the decisions and contact is difficult with other group members ... Many people have not shown up since the first week and have no way of contact. These people obviously don't want to be committed, but no one knows for sure.

Facilitator
The facilitator for VOYCE is an education officer and a member of Brighton Council's Environmental Services Education Group, made up of officers from a number of different departments, including Community Health, Town Planning, Countryside Services, Cemeteries and Crematorium. The youth group has benefited from the work done by the facilitator and her colleagues on an

environmental education pack, *Learning about your Environment* (Brighton Borough Council, 1993). This is a collection of information, educational material and advice from various council departments. The information is well presented and easily accessible for young people, providing an excellent starting point for the group's efforts. It contains documents produced by the Council, such as its 'Charter for the Environment', explains complicated terms, gives facts and figures, suggests techniques for investigations and environmental monitoring and acts as a focus and stimulus to explore environmental issues. The facilitator for VOYCE is the first point of contact group members have with the Council and a link with other council officers. She alerts the group to local issues, helps them identify opportunities to participate and enables them to develop ways of working together. Her enthusiastic support has helped the group maintain its momentum.

Comment

In attempting to alert others to environmental issues, particularly those concerned with the use of resources, members of VOYCE have learnt a great deal about the environment. They have also learnt how the local authority deals with environmental matters and how the public thinks. Through the efforts of the group's facilitator, they are able to understand more fully the role of local authority officers and elected members. The young people are also more aware of the importance of media coverage and publicity to disseminate ideas and opinions and to create local interest and support. The skills they have learnt in organising their group will transfer to other situations. It is likely that they will develop the motivation to play an active part in local environmental issues in the future, bringing benefit to the local authority.

CASE STUDY 3 **Devon Youth Council
Next Generation Project** Age 14–18+

This example describes the work of a county youth forum, which is well resourced, has a high profile in the local authority and is funded by the council. It describes the efforts of young people to engage others in exploring environmental issues through drama and performance.

The Devon Youth Council developed from the Devon Year for Youth in 1991. It is a pressure group for young people's rights led by young people themselves.

It is based in the Local Agenda 21 office at the County Hall and receives funding from a number of departments, mainly Education. Its budget of £22,000 funds a coordinator (salary £6000) and the expenses of 20 elected members of the Youth Council, which reports to the Council's community services committee. It is regularly consulted on the day-to-day business of local authority departments and invited to participate in significant events. It was invited to contribute to the planning of the commemoration of the fiftieth anniversary of Victory in Europe. The young people wanted it to have a long-term impact which would influence people's attitudes to war. The group was also invited to form a youth Roundtable in response to Agenda 21, but members felt that although young people wanted to make their views on the environment known, this was not the most appropriate way to seek opinions. They saw a possible link between the need to address concerns highlighted by Local Agenda 21 and the experience of the war. During the Second World War, communities had worked together and sacrificed much to win against a common enemy. The common enemy now, in their view, was potential environmental disaster.

Project
The Youth Council suggested that the arts was a popular and appropriate medium for young people to explore complex ideas. A proposal for the 'Next Generation' Project was developed, supported by the Agenda 21 team of the Devon Environment Department, together with the County Environment Director and the local education authority.

The Next Generation Project was an attempt to:

• promote the Devon Youth Council

• enable young people to be more artistically aware

• inform young people about the Second World War and its consequences

• inform and activate young people around environmental issues

• give young people the opportunity to express their opinions and ideas

The idea was to create an interactive piece of entertainment which could be performed in schools and youth clubs. A specialist in theatre in education was appointed to manage the day-to-day running of the project and guide the production. Five unemployed youths and theatre arts students from Dartington College of Arts made up the rest of the team.

Planning involved a period of research and development of the ideas where the greatest benefit was from talking to people who had experience of the issues. Two theatre in education performances and workshops were developed, 'Celebration' and 'Everybody's Child'. There were 11 performances in schools and youth centres, comprising monologues and duologues, some focusing on the Second World War, others featuring elderly people recalling their experience. The characters became involved with the audience, challenging them and engaging them in discussion, about peace, the future, the role of young people in society and the environment. In the workshops, audience members were given the opportunity to define their own social and environmental priorities. In the weeks following the performances, video recordings were made of participants' responses to the performances. These were edited to produce a presentation at the Celebration Day. After a performance in the morning, a 'question time' debate with representatives from the County Council was chaired by the Youth Council in the afternoon. This covered key environmental issues including waste disposal, recycling, cryptosporidium in water supplies, public transport and the impact and effects of modern farming techniques.

Evaluation
Students who had performed felt that the audiences had gained a better understanding of issues which were previously vague and that they had explored new ways to communicate theatre in education practices and theories. It was evident that they had learnt much from repeating the show over a sustained period and had managed to achieve good levels of communication without an obvious authority figure directing. The project coordinator thought that the performances had been generally well received. Topics had informed and challenged a broader range of people than had originally been intended, especially the students who had performed. He observed that the young people who had participated were more interested in and creatively energised by Agenda 21 issues than by the subject of VE Day. However, creating links between the past, present and future and encouraging young people to think deeply about environmental and community issues had made a difference in the thinking of young people.

Next stage
In the next stage of the project, the plan is to establish a Devon Young People's Agenda 21 Roundtable, comprising a country-wide team of young people to represent the interests of the county's youth on Local Agenda 21 issues. As a means of contributing to the discussion, a Local Action roadshow is planned to tour school and youth groups, and introduce young people to Agenda 21. The aim is to encourage discussion about the actions which individuals might take to promote sustainable development.

CHAPTER 7 **Research**

Opportunities to contribute to a vision for change have been stimulated by young people's involvement in research through responding to question-naires or participating in research projects in other ways. Drama, storytelling, poetry, group interviews, diaries and photographic journals are techniques which can be used to generate qualitative data on children's experiences, perceptions and opinions.

Young people have become involved in environmental issues through research projects initiated by a variety of agencies, such as local authorities, non-governmental agencies and universities. The impetus comes from a wish to consult young people about their experience or perceptions of the environment, or perhaps find out about their needs or aspirations. In helping to collect data about their route to school, the use of the neighbourhood for play activities or their views on the nature of town centres, they are able to contribute to the planning and development process. They can provide information which would be difficult to collect in other ways. If the research is well handled, there can be educational benefits which will transfer to other settings. Young people are encouraged to think about environmental issues, to identify what the problems are and to start to think about how they might be addressed. In carrying out the surveys or contributing to the research process, they sometimes realise that there are no easy answers to environmental problems and that judgements and decisions need to be based on evidence. Research projects have also helped to provide materials for environmental education.

The educational value of the exercise for the children must be clear. Otherwise there is the danger of using children as research fodder, as a means of generating research material on the cheap, as publicity opportunities for commercial firms or public relations for local government. Work with children as researchers needs to be carefully thought out to ensure the reliability of the data. In school-based research, researchers do not always appreciate the extra burden for teachers which dealing with questionnaires can create.

This report demonstrates how professional research can not only involve young people as respondents, but can also act as a stimulus for children to become researchers themselves. Their own investigations result in a fuller understanding of environmental issues and they are able to participate in planning issues with increased knowledge and greater confidence.

The Department of Landscape at the University at Sheffield was the base for a two-year programme investigating children's use and perception of their town centres. The research was structured around the *Futuretown* education pack (Miller, 1994) sponsored by Boots the Chemist and Marks and Spencer in March, 1994. The pack was one expression of concern for the future of town centres held by these particular retailers. A second year of the education programme, 'Futuretown II', has been sponsored by Boots the Chemist and Sainsbury's. The research project was funded by the Economic and Social Research Council.

Aims of research
The main aims of the research were:

- to identify the current level of use that children make of their town centres

- to identify who children go to town with, or meet there, why they go and what activities and behaviours they engage in when they are there

- to identify whether children go to other urban places not in the town centre, such as out of town shopping centres and if so, why they go there

- to identify what might elicit more positive behavioural responses to town centre environments from children

- to make recommendations relating to ways in which town centres can be made more attractive to children and so elicit positive responses from them, to assist the reversal of the current downward spiral of many such places

Strategies for participation
The *Futuretown* pack was targeted at eight schools, four primary and four secondary, in each of 60 towns throughout the United Kingdom. It was decided that the research team would initially try to obtain responses from a sample of children in four schools, two primary and two secondary, in 15 towns.

A questionnaire entitled 'You and your town centre' was designed to be attractive to children and to encourage them to complete it. It took the form of an A4 booklet with computer-generated graphics. Questions were grouped into sections entitled 'Questions about you', 'Going into the town centre', 'Your town', 'Other places' and 'The future'.

Teachers who agreed to be involved were sent two sets of questionnaires, one for use before undertaking the Futuretown Project and one for use afterwards. This was to test whether children's use and perception of town centres had changed after exposure to the pack. Notes were also supplied to teachers to explain how to use the questionnaire.

Problems

Finance and resources obviously limited and constrained the research project. It would have been ideal if all the schools could have been studied where the *Futuretown* pack was used, but this was not possible. Thus a layered sampling structure of towns, schools and number of pupils within each school was adopted. Time also proved to be a constraint, in terms of matching the research needs with those of the school year. It took time to identify schools, prepare questionnaires, structure the research programme and develop the work in schools.

One of the biggest logistical problems encountered during this work was that of discovering which schools were actually involved with the *Futuretown* education pack. Researchers made personal contact with the schools, and letters and telephone calls paved the way for each school's involvement in the research. Despite the fact that everything was done to ensure the return of completed questionnaires, there was still a lot of chasing up by letter and telephone required for the return of the information.

Outcomes

The main outcome has been the production of a significant amount of data relating to children's use of and perception of their local town centres, other local towns and out-of-town shopping developments. This is being disseminated in a variety of academic and professional publications and has received significant press coverage, including BBC Radio 4's *Women's Hour*. The work has been reported in the *Futuretown Newsletter*, the Boots report on the Futuretown Project and the ESRC Annual Report. Another welcome outcome is that some of the schools who participated in the research found that their involvement had an educational value. Two schools reported that pupils had learnt about the use of questionnaires from the research. They had modelled their own on those supplied by the researchers. Other schools reported that children had done projects involving mapping and the design of their town centre. In Harlow, the research questionnaire was used as a basis for public consultation in the redevelopment of the town centre south area. In Harlow and Ellesmere Port, it was also used as a basis for consultation for their Single Regeneration bids.

On reflection

The research was very enjoyable and much information about children's perceptions and use of their local town centres was collected. It was surprising and exciting how much interest could be generated by trying to understand in greater detail people's use and perceptions of their urban environments. The research revealed how much money children declared they spent on their last visit to the town centre, the perception that Liverpool, for example, is liked but also feared, the attraction of out-of-town shopping centres have for young people and complaints about litter. It was evident from teachers' responses that the *Futuretown* pack had been of significant value to some schools as a method of raising awareness about issues relating to the future of town centres. However, this was not clear from differences in responses to the first and second questionnaire, as there was perhaps not enough time to identify any significant changes in children's perceptions of their behaviours. During the second year of the project, researchers have returned to some of the schools to undertake focus group discussions with pupils to develop a deeper understanding of their feelings. Some of this information will be used to inform town centre managers, planners and other professionals involved in town centre design and development. The benefit for the commercial sponsors was that they had feedback from potential customers and users of town centres which would have been difficult to access in other ways.

Comment

Many pupils benefited from their involvement in this research, which helped them to think about issues relating to town centre development and to learn the use of particular research techniques. Schools are under great pressure these days and it is not always possible for teachers to respond to requests from researchers, especially where they are asked to act as research assistants in helping to collect data. It is not easy to justify pupils' involvement, accommodate research activities within the curriculum at the time required, or create the time to deal with it. However, if there is a clear educational benefit for the pupils, it is more likely that teachers will respond enthusiastically.

CASE STUDY 5	**Liverpool 8**	
	Children's Needs Survey	Age 7–11

This case study describes how children contributed to a research programme and how adults sought to develop appropriate instruments for research into children's perceptions of their environment, using questionnaires, poetry and drama.

Background

In 1992, the South West Toxteth Liaison Committee, a group of Liverpool City Council elected members, officers and voluntary sector representatives, proposed that the Education Department undertake a survey of the needs of children living in the Granby, Abercrombie and Dingle Wards. The City Council play officer in the Education Department discussed how to do this with The Children's Society, which had a project based in Liverpool 8. It was agreed that:

- the methods and form of research must enable children's needs and concerns to be heard

- local organisations should be involved in the research

- the research should evolve into action research to achieve positive change for children

- policy-makers should be persuaded to include children in decision-making processes that shape their communities

Liverpool 8 Children's Research Group

In 1993, local organisations, together with representatives of the Parents' Support Programme and the City Council, formed the Liverpool 8 Children's Research Group, which remained in operation until March 1997. Organisational and administrative support was provided by The Children's Society and the City Council neighbourhood play development worker. The research was inevitably influenced by the qualities of the members, their skills, knowledge and values, and also by the context in which the group operated, an area of social and economic deprivation, its problems compounded by the impact of racism. There was a concern that the results of the research should lead to action. The research programme was funded by The Children's Society, the John Moores Foundation, the Baring Foundation and Liverpool City Council. Granby Management Development Agency undertook the pilot survey, supervised by Priority Focus, a consultancy group.

Pilot study

As a means of developing appropriate methods of research, both quantitative and qualitative, the group undertook a number of pilot projects. 'Priority Search', a computer-aided research method, was used for a questionnaire involving 129 children aged 7–11 from Beaufort Street and Granby Street Schools. The question 'What could we do to make your community a better place?' was given to a focus group of children in each of these schools and they were asked to provide 'solutions'. Two-hour sessions took place in each school with representative groups of children. They provided 38 solutions, which were included in the main questionnaire to be ranked by the children in order of priority. A similar amount of time was allowed to enable children to complete the questionnaire. This also included a data fieldsheet which enabled the results to be analysed in terms of age, gender and school.

The intention was that the report derived from this initial survey would form the basis for the much larger piece of research, using different methods, aimed at promoting the voice of children in the decision-making processes that affected their lives and futures in their community. The basis of this further phase of research was a questionnaire.

Questionnaire

The questionnaire was completed by a total of 555 children in response to the question, 'What would you do to improve the area where you live?' The responses fell into categories, focusing on safety, caring for others, a friendly and fairer world and environmental concerns. The main issues which the children identified were concerned with their personal safety and the safety of the wider community. Their acute social awareness emerged as a key consideration in the research findings. Bullying was identified as an issue. The researchers thought that the children's concern about the danger of drugs and guns was perhaps exacerbated by local and national media coverage. Empty houses and pollution were perceived as distressing and linked with drug abusers and discarded needles.

The researchers felt that the survey demonstrated that a process which is participatory provides a clearer identification of need and one which reflects more accurately children's perspectives of their world. The intention was that the findings should be used as a tool for action by the Liverpool 8 Research Group and others who should then make recommendations, addressed to those who work with children and policy-makers, which could be used to bring about positive change for children.

Problems

The Liverpool City Council play officer reported on the practical difficulties of carrying out a survey with children and admitted that it was not as simple as it first appeared. Although the focus group had helped to shape the questionnaire, when it was given to the full group, there were problems with children's understanding of so many items (31 on the data field-sheet and 38 on the questionnaire) and difficulties in making responses. Children may also have been limited by their own experience in relation to what they could propose, and some responses may have been influenced by other children.

There was also some confusion between children's needs and their desires. Although the exercise had been labelled 'Children's Needs Survey', the results could be construed as a kind of wish list. Children wanted 'Camelot and Pleasure Island, theme parks, less pollution, free cinemas, no more smoking, roller dome, people to be nice, zebra crossings, more jobs, streets to be tidied, fairground and fun house, more computers, sports centres, swimming pool, more school outings and more houses'. There were differences in preferences between girls and boys, between children of different age group and between the two schools.

Comment

The question arose as to whether a questionnaire was an appropriate medium to elicit the information required. Children's written responses might not necessarily reveal a full picture. It might not encourage serious reflection and a proper consideration of children's needs. The format of a questionnaire requires summary judgements and does not allow children to analyse or evaluate their present experience as a basis for identifying the need for change, or to express any nuances or subtle interpretations. The compilation of a 'shopping list' as possible suggestions for change may suggest to children that problems are capable of quick-fix solutions. In relation to the notion of participation, we might question whether the use of questionnaires is an appropriate way to involve children. They may not understand the part this plays in the wider process of consultation and planning, and the quality of the information elicited may not be useful for informing policy or future research.

Poetry workshops, drama sessions and neighbourhood walks

Poetry sessions and neighbourhood walks also took place with children from Mossview School in Partington, an area of Trafford. Children's voices, photographs and poems were recorded. Members of the research group, together with a teacher, parents and Somali bilingual workers, devised and ran drama sessions with children aged 4–11 in Granby Street School. These sessions were based on the theme of visitors from space asking children about their lives, how they played and where they lived. They were recorded using tape recorders, photographs and 'space' notebooks. In addition, children were asked to draw pictures about 'three wishes', concerned with what they would like to be, and what they would like to play. A group of children was also asked to keep a diary for a week. A worker from The Children's Society together with a member of the Catalyst Drama Group ran drama sessions during a summer play scheme at the Methodist Centre in Granby. Through these pilot projects, the research group was able to develop a programme for the main piece of research carried out in 1995 and 1996.

The Windows Poetry Group worked for two-hour sessions with groups of children to generate, through children's poetry, qualitative information about their lives. Poetry writing sessions resulted in an excellent range of illuminative writing. The collection of poems, *It Makes Me Mad*, expressed the children's feelings, revealing positive and negative experience. The children's words spoke for children everywhere, yet also suggested a particular sense of place. Much of this described the children's environment, conjuring up a vivid picture of the neighbourhood. Poems mentioned the sights, sounds and smells which the children experienced: 'roof top clouds, fingers full of wind, face full of sun', 'mishy soil', 'bottles and bags everywhere', 'crisp packets and old lemonade cans litter the pavements and gutters', 'cars zooming past every second', 'sabotaged cars abandoned and burned'. They described the people they encountered: 'drunken men swingle past', 'I play with my brother and get into trouble with my mother', 'loads of people shouting and screaming'. They tell of their activities: 'we play on the swings', 'I play in my den', ' I play in the cemetery', 'nowhere to play, nothing to do'.

There was an interesting and significant difference between the poems produced by the children in Liverpool 8 and those in Partington, an area that bordered open countryside. Though there were some celebratory poems, those from Liverpool 8 placed a greater emphasis on social problems such as violence, drugs and guns, on relationships and the lack of play space. By contrast, the poems from Partington focused strongly on a celebration of nature.

Results
The poetry workshops were perhaps a more subtle and effective way of generating responses which tapped into children's experiences and revealed their perceptions. A key aspect of the consultation process in this case study, both through the development of the questionnaire and through the poetry work-

shops, was that children were asked to generate ideas as to the form of the research, rather than merely respond to an adult agenda which had already been determined.

The Liverpool Research Group was amazed at the competence of many of the children who took part and moved by the relevance of their observations to real events, such as the Dunblane massacre. They noticed a consistency between the results obtained using different methods, through a qualitative approach by means of poetry and drama and a more quantitative emphasis through Priority Search. Interpreting the results, the Liverpool 8 Children's Research Group learnt that:

- Children were knowledgeable and able to express their views.

- They were concerned about social relationships.

- They presented a powerful moral statement to adults about the condition of society in general and their community in particular.

- The children presented a political statement to adults, going beyond the 'participation, consultation and rights' agenda.

- Age was not a barrier. Children were physically in touch with their environment. They were enthusiastic and optimistic about change.

- The results of the research could be used to set down a marker for future work and to assess policy-making.

CHAPTER 8 Local plans, urban development plans

M any local authority officers have been able to use opportunities created by regeneration initiatives, the City Challenge Programme, local plans, urban development plans and unitary development plans to promote a greater interest in environmental and planning issues. In some instances, their involvement has represented a considerable investment of time, expertise and other resources. The question arises as to how the benefit of this investment might be maximised to provide an enriched experience for young people.

One way of using this new investment is to produce educational materials drawing on information and resources which already exist in various local authority departments and adapting them for use in schools and youth organisations. However, this requires effort from a dedicated person or an interdisciplinary team to ensure they are disseminated and help to strengthen a local environmental education network. Linked to this may be opportunities for professional development, where teachers, youth workers, environmental, design and community professionals can come together to share their expertise to devise strategies which will empower young people through education for participation. The working contact with professionals other than teachers has extended and enriched what can happen in the schools. Children's views have been given attention and their work has been publicly valued. Education has been taken into the public arena and the workings of the local authority held up to scrutiny by the children.

In the main, the impetus has come from planning departments, though sometimes leisure services or arts have taken the initiative. Local authority officers have extended consultation procedures and have experimented with a variety of approaches to include children and young people, encouraging them to articulate their particular concerns. What is not always clear is who is listening and what the mechanisms are for influencing the decision-makers. The worry is that presentations to elected members and the publicity in local newspapers might create a flurry of interest, but have no long-term impact on the way we plan environments to accommodate young people.

CASE STUDY 6   **Birmingham City Council
Erdington Local Action Plan**   Age 10

Birmingham City Council is an example of a local authority committed to involving young people in education for participation. The case study reports on a project which developed over several months through which children were able to make a contribution to the development of Erdington's Local Action Plan. The experience helped them to understand issues relating to urban planning and decision-making. Features of the project were studies of local history, townscape appraisal, site analysis and illumination of the planning process.

The Department of Planning and Architecture at Birmingham City Council has undertaken an impressive number of initiatives over recent years as part of its commitment to working with young people on planning issues affecting their locality. The director of the Planning and Architecture Department believes that, 'It is important not only for children to understand the history that is around them, but also to begin to understand how their environment is managed, what forces there are that are trying to change it and how the people, through government, can control these pressures and direct them in a beneficial way. As planners in local government, we need an educated public to take an interest in what is going on'. Birmingham's development plan, which sets the context for much of the department's work, has as its primary aim 'to provide a social, cultural and physical environment which allows all groups to play a satisfying and distinctive part in the life of the city'. Children and young people are seen as a significant group.

Birmingham City Council entered into partnership with Community Service Volunteers, the sponsoring agency, in late 1994 to promote 'Citizen 2000', a three-year nationwide programme. The aim of the scheme was to allow young people to have a stake in the future of the city by being actively involved in their local communities and the work of the City Council. The Department of Architecture and Planning pledged itself to incorporating a Citizen 2000 scheme as part of preparing a Local Action Plan for Erdington, an area to the north of the city centre. One of the aims of the Citizen 2000 project was to encourage and enable young people to participate in setting an agenda, carry out survey work, explore environmental issues and make proposals.

Citizen 2000, Osborne School

In 1995, 30 ten-year-olds from Osborne Junior and Infant School were invited to participate in a programme of activities focusing on 'Our neighbourhood' and 'Our future'. This was designed by the Community Education Department and the Department of Planning and Architecture with the aim of ensuring the children had sufficient background knowledge and understanding of their area and the process of town planning. Over a seven-month period, the pupils explored local history and the development of the area, focusing on conservation issues, particularly new uses for old buildings (see Figure 4). The starting point, local history research, was organised by the local studies centre of the Central Library, where the group worked on archive material, old photographs and ordnance survey maps illustrating evolution and change in Erdington.

Figure 4 Pupils from Osborne School discuss work with the local studies librarian on archive material which illustrates evolution and change in Erdington

Visits

A session with a planning officer was organised to introduce the Action Plan and explain why it was needed and how it was produced. A prominent vacant site in Erdington was then explored as a potential subject of a planning application. The children visited the site to undertake a site analysis. This involved measuring the site and recording surrounding land uses. They carried out an appraisal of the high street shopping centre, taking into account its accessibility and functions, and made an appraisal of building materials. Site visits and project work followed, including traffic counts, building and townscape appraisals. Some role play was undertaken to help participants understand the difficulties which people in wheelchairs, parents with pushchairs or blind people might experience. One child said, 'I was a baby in a pushchair for the day. Some of the kerbs had been lowered which made the ride smoother and some of the doorways in the shops were wide with no steps, which helped us get in and out more easily. The cracks in the pavements were troublesome and the pedestrian crossings only allowed us four seconds to get across. We didn't like the dog mess on the pavement' (*Osborne Echo*, April 1995).

Development

The children formulated proposals for the development of the site and discussed these with the planning officer. This activity was completed with children voting by holding up cards saying 'SHOULD' and 'SHOULDN'T'. One of the children commented, 'We really liked this activity because it helped us understand the way that decisions are made in Erdington. Martin helped us look at the consequences of decisions and how these things affect local people and their businesses' (*Osborne Echo*, April 1995). Visits were made to the Department of Planning and Architecture and the Council House, where the children experimented with computer-aided design. They learned what happens to a planning application and found out about the role of elected members and what happens in the Council Chamber. The principal planning officer felt that the activities which worked best were those which had a practical feel to them. For instance, one seminar which he coordinated involved six architects and planners visiting the school to discuss issues including the use of building materials in listed buildings and meeting the needs of disabled people, which led to a role play exercise.

Outcomes

The project culminated in a community launch with the local MP, chief officers, committee chairs and local ward members, at which the children presented their proposals and exhibited their work. The children's views will be incorporated in the Planning and Architecture Department's public consultation newsletter which will be distributed to local people as part of a wider consultation exercise. The school is being kept in touch via feedback sessions, so they are fully informed on the progress of their suggestions. Draft copies of the plan will be displayed at the school, with an invitation for further comments to be made prior to the plan being finalised. This is the first project of its kind and Birmingham City Council hopes to run similar exercises when preparing other local action plans.

Evaluation

The deputy headteacher commented that the most effective learning came when the children were engaged in practical learning activities. Teachers appreciated the cross-curricular nature of the work and saw positive educational benefits from a community-oriented project which had meaning for the children. The principal planning officer thought, 'The project with Osborne School has been mutually rewarding. As well as children learning about town planning, we as a department have learnt what changes our youngest citizens would like to see in their neighbourhood'. He emphasised that the success of the project reflected the cooperation and goodwill between all the parties involved.

Comment

Two aims of helping children to understand the planning process and enabling them to contribute to the development of a local plan were addressed by the project at Osborne Junior and Infant School. Although this account gives very little description of the development of the work in the school, it was a comprehensive programme, and the children benefited greatly from the experience. Particularly important were the site visits and the development of appropriate techniques for townscape appraisal. Children were able to engage in debate about complex issues at their own level, considering conservation, the use of building materials and access for disabled people.

The project reflects the local authority's major commitment to education for participation. What was significant was the degree of effort made by the Planning and Architecture Department to engage young people in the challenging and exciting process of environmental change. This was not a one-off initiative, but followed on from other educational activities which the department has organised. The concern is that young people understand the nature of the planning process so that their judgements can be better informed. The long-term aim is to develop a public more able to engage in planning matters.

CASE STUDY 7   **Brecon Beacons National Park Planning For Real**   Age 7–11

After initial concerns and reservations about involving children in a consultative process, a productive relationship developed between a primary school and a Local Plan team. The school and children benefited from an input of resources and expertise. The Local Plan team gained a new perspective on the involvement of children in decision-making.

Planning for Real

'Planning for Real' is a consultation technique which encourages people to express their ideas about how they would like to see their local area developed. Using a large-scale model of the area and an informal public meeting, Planning for Real exercises can combine first-hand local knowledge with expert advice from professionals. The outcomes may feature in various contexts: in a planning brief, local plan, or in bids for government schemes. Planning for Real is a registered trademark of the Neighbourhood Initiative Foundation, Telford.

Consultation

In 1992, the Brecon Beacons National Park Authority initiated a process for producing its park-wide Local Plan using the Planning for Real method. At that time, public relations were considered to be poor and the technique set up by Local Plan teams was developed in the hope of being able to win the trust and support of local people. The initiative was developed first with adult groups and then as an 'accidental by-product' with children.

In 1993, 39 meetings were held to cover all the communities in the National Park. It was considered impractical to construct 40 models to represent the different localities, so use of a newly installed geographical information system, 'MapInfo', enabled the production of large-scale coloured maps mounted on polystyrene tiles. The large scale made it easier for people not used to interpreting maps to read the maps and even locate their own house and garden. A series of posters was also provided to guide the discussion towards particularly relevant issues that the Local Plan would need to address. These included information on housing, employment, transport, tourism, environment and community. Residents were asked to respond to questions on the posters and indicate areas on the maps relating to these issues.

The sorts of questions being posed to the group related to a range of issues and themes. Did the area need more housing? Were there places in need of environmental improvement? Were there sites that needed protecting and conserving? The group responded by placing coloured pins, flags and 'monopoly' houses on to their map and a strong visual display of the issues emerged. This exercise was followed by a more formal discussion with any consensus, compromise or opposing view written on a flip chart in full view of the audience.

The exercise was considered successful, in that participation rates were high, and many residents who would not normally have had the confidence to speak out to a platform of professionals were drawn to speak as the discussion developed.

School's involvement

The headteacher of Gilwern School, Abergavenny, was approached by the team to hire out her school hall for one of the adult sessions. She said she would allow them free use of it if they would run the exercise with children in the school. It was, in her view, an 'ideal opportunity for the children to interact with their environment and most importantly to make their learning real'.

There was a concerned reaction from the parties involved. The National Park officers had reservations. The planners were concerned about the Local Plan policies being dictated by children's views and the education officer was not sure whether the issues would be fully understood by children.

However, once committed, time was spent in preparing strategies for the session and resourcing it appropriately (see Figure 5). With the help of the Park's education officer, there was discussion with the children beforehand on the planner's role, how the village might develop, what the children particularly liked and disliked and how they would like to see the village change. The headteacher explained that the children had all written essays for the National Park's education officer, which he used to prepare the session. The children's version of Planning for Real was developed, based on the same process as the adult meetings. Questions posed to the children focused particularly on the immediate school environment, maintenance issues, provision for litter, lighting, as well as facilities for the village and what children would like to see there.

The children's reactions were very positive. The Local Plan team's report comments, 'It became clear that the children not only understood the concept and the mechanics of the technique but also enjoyed taking part in it'. The young people involved indicated a sound grasp of the issues and generated ideas relating to all sectors of the community: 'a safe place to cross the road on my route to school, more shops for old people who haven't got cars, houses for people who have just got married and haven't got much money but want to stay in the village'.

Figure 5 Pupils at Gilwern School take part in a Planning for Real exercise as part of the consultation programme to consider the development of the Brecon Beacons National Park

At the session, a group of the children expressed an interest in the posters being prepared for an adult meeting later that day. They spent time discussing amongst themselves material from the posters on sheltered housing, community facilities and traffic calming and 'with limited prompting, developed a vision for the village with a consensus that was sadly lacking in some of the adults who attended the evening meeting'.

As it happened, the children's and adults' sessions overlapped and as adults arrived, some were a little perturbed to see the children involved. The head-teacher commented, 'We didn't rush the children out and there was some interaction between the groups. It seems to me that the children's responses were far more informed. They have a streetwise knowledge of the village that the adults don't have, probably because of car use. The children are much more open minded and more aware of environmental problems in the village'.

Comment

What emerges from the report on this consultation process is not only an honest acknowledgement of the initial concerns and reservations about working with children from some of the professionals involved, but a considerable reappraisal based on the experience. The initiative was recognised as important for its role in education for participation 'because of the strong community decision-making ethos of the technique, the children were experiencing at an early age skills which will stand them in good stead as they grow up'.

In her evaluation, the headteacher expressed the view that there are many benefits from this sort of initiative, not least of which was the beautifully produced resource material and a huge map of the village which filled a third of the school hall. 'The children really enjoyed it and it made me realise just how much they like living in this village. They also felt really valued by David Brinn [Brecon Beacons National Park education officer]. It did their confidence a lot of good'.

This approach is currently being extended to develop a collaborative project between the Park's education officer and the Local Plans officer. The focus for this initiative is to introduce the concept of sustainable development using debating and decision-making skills based on the Planning for Real techniques. 'Sustainability for Real' is being piloted with a number of primary schools.

| CASE STUDY 8 | **Leicester City Council** | |
| | **Traffic Calming Project** | Age 8–11 |

This case study reports on work developed through a partnership between Children Today Leicestershire, Leicester City Council and community groups. This represented a considerable investment of resources to develop a consultation programme aimed at improving safety on three city streets. Aims were to develop a consultation process accessible to both children and adults and to gain support for public policies. This process involved a range of techniques including questionnaires, interviews, exhibitions and meetings in a variety of venues, with Council officers working across departmental boundaries.

If one of the most accessible places for children to play is near to their home, in city areas this will often mean local streets. As little as 30 years ago this was nothing remarkable. Photographs taken at the time show children of all ages playing on the pavements and in the road space. This is certainly not the case in the same streets in the 1990s, largely dominated by traffic and parked cars.

The danger that these increased levels of traffic represent, the lack of people and other perceived threats to children's safety, have combined to increase restrictions not only on children's play but also on their general mobility and independence. Research suggests that in 1971, 80 per cent of seven- and eight-year-olds were allowed to go to school on their own. By 1990, this figure had dropped to 9 per cent (Hillman, 1990).

Children Today

In 1990 the National Children's Play and Recreation Unit, supported by the Department of National Heritage, set up 'Children Today', a development programme aimed at exploring provision of play opportunities for children. Project teams were set up in Devon, the North West and Leicestershire to work in partnership with voluntary groups, local authority officers and play officers to promote better coordinated services. Children Today Leicestershire has identified traffic as a major restriction on children's mobility and opportunity for play. An exciting venture in the city of Leicester is attempting to tackle the traffic problem in an imaginative way. Leicester City Council is working towards a street play policy by bringing together engineers, housing officers, parks and play officers and members of the Planning Department.

Consultation

In 1990, the Department of Transport set a target to reduce traffic casualties by one third by the year 2000. They have released funds to local authorities to be spent on traffic calming in order to reach this target. For Children Today Leicestershire, this seemed a real opportunity to improve streets for children as well as adults, ensuring that children's play needs were highlighted. Children Today set up the Street Play Project, aiming to make three city streets, one with a small play area, safer and more interesting for children's play. Door-to-door interviews were organised by playworkers, residents and interpreters to ask local people their views of the project. Two public meetings were also held to explain the project and issues involved. A group of residents, including children, began work on preparing the consultation process with officers from Engineering Services, Leisure Services, Planning, Housing and a design consultancy, Archaid.

Much of the first year was spent by Children Today Leicestershire raising awareness of the project with relevant City Council officers and other organisations. An application for Urban Programme funding was made to pay for modifications to the streets, and additional small sums were provided by Leicester City Council. A number of initiatives were organised to keep local people informed and involved. Two newsletters were circulated to all residents and an outdoor exhibition was commissioned to explain 'traffic calming' and the range of possible changes. Soft Touch Community Arts mounted a weatherproof exhibition outside the local school and in the streets, with panels at child and adult height (see Figure 6). It showed pictures of street designs, ramps, paving, trees and ideas for the play area, with City Council officers on hand to answer questions. According to the Children Today report, it attracted large numbers of adults and children over much shorter periods than similar exhibitions housed indoors.

Figure 6 Parents concerned for the safety of their children consider plans for the Street Play Project in Leicester, on view in the street as a weatherproof exhibition organised by Soft Touch Community Arts Co-op. Photo courtesy of Soft Touch Community Arts, Leicester

Two sessions were held in the school to give children and adults the opportunity to communicate their own ideas; street surveys were also carried out. The resulting 38-item questionnaire was delivered to every household, with interpreters for Asian residents whose first language was not English. According to the report, the questionnaires could take up to an hour to complete, but that contact time helped build good links. A really concerted effort was made to reach the community in this project. To help people who preferred to visualize possible changes rather than complete a questionnaire, Soft Touch made 1:72 scale models of the three streets and play area, personalised by pasting photographs of the actual houses on to the fronts. Four sessions were held using the models. The report states, 'Children tended to make things they wanted to see, adults used the model as a focus for discussion. Both worked together and communicated more than at any other stage of the consultation'.

Development of ideas
The next stage was for the design team to pull together the range of comments and form a realistic brief. This part of the process was described in the report as perhaps the hardest part of all, with many often contradictory comments. The team focused on the more realistic and affordable ideas and were able to translate some of the concerns reflected in participants' ideas into physical changes. Their design attempted to fulfil the aim of slowing traffic, increasing the amount of space available for children and incorporating items of play value while enabling residents to continue to use and park their cars. The draft plans included ramps at either end of the streets, a 12-metre speed table or elongated ramp in the middle of each street and extended pavements to allow only one lane of traffic. Coloured paving designs, trees, decorative bars and cemented-in boulders were used on the extended pavements. If sufficient funding is available, a sign or decorative archway will indicate to drivers they are entering a residential area where children play. The outdoor exhibition was used again to show residents the draft plans and receive their comments.

The overall cost of consultation, design and construction, excluding most staff costs, was approximately £90,000 for three streets and one play area. The primary funding source was the Urban Programme, providing £64,100. The remaining contribution came from City Council Departments of Housing, Leisure Services and Engineering. The report highlighted the fact that as a pilot or demonstration project, this is more expensive than work as part of an ordinary programme and that work utilising traffic calming funds focusing on children's play needs will not normally include a play area. The report suggests that street designs like this one could at relatively modest cost form part of future traffic calming schemes, though further evaluative work needs to take place to assess the impact on children's play potential and the long-term response of the residents. 'Only when this evaluation is done, with repeated local consultation, can progress be made and future traffic calming money really benefit the quarter of Leicester's citizens who are children.'

Comment

Members of Children Today Leicestershire have made a number of interesting recommendations as a result of this project. They not only emphasise the importance of consulting children when making changes to streets or play areas but assert that consultation saves time and money in the long run. The team spent nearly three months and much thought and effort devising a consultation process which would be accessible to both children and adults. However, the actual consultation process took less than two weeks, using existing City Council staff, offering almost all households in the three streets an opportunity to participate and generating a representative range of responses. It was important that children were involved as they are the people who benefit most from traffic calming measures. The report concludes 'people felt they had been asked. Such exercises can build better relationships and stronger support for public policies across a city or county'.

This was a well considered programme to engage the local community, including children, in the consultation process. It involved a range of techniques, including questionnaires, interviews, exhibitions and meetings in a variety of locations. It also involved officers working across departmental boundaries. It represented a huge investment of resources. However, the City Council thought that this was money well spent, as it increased the likelihood of the environmental changes being understood and welcomed by the residents.

CHAPTER 9   Urban regeneration

The issue of urban regeneration and the involvement of local people in consultation programmes is a feature of local authority work nationwide. It is also a potential focus for community projects involved in working with young people and interdisciplinary teams of environment professionals committed to involving children in environmental change. An awareness exists amongst all these groups that children and young people's needs are not taken into account when consultation programmes are planned and that there is little or no opportunity for their views to be heard.

For local authorities, involving young people in making their contribution to urban regeneration initiatives represents investment of already stretched resources, so it may be limited to those who are committed to its importance. As part of this, planners and other local authority officers can help young people explore the complexities of development proposals and generate their own ideas, as well as provide insight into conflicts of interest in the local community.

There are other agencies, particularly community projects, involved in the promotion of young people's participation in environmental change and it is clear that they offer a range of skills for engaging children and young people. They can create settings within which young people can be encouraged to think and take action for themselves. It is when these agencies work in collaboration with other sectors, or in multidisciplinary partnerships, that these opportunities can be maximised. In this context, young people are offered learning experiences which extend their understanding and skills, and their responses to issues which affect them are listened to and valued.

What remains unclear is how this process might be maintained and developed in the long term, in particular to maximise young people's involvement in thinking and taking action for themselves. The long-term benefits for the community of equipping young people with these 'stewardship' skills requires more widespread acknowledgement and support.

CASE STUDY 9 **Patio Estate, Rotherham Consultation Project** Age 3–8

The work of the Patio Project shows how it is possible to engage young children in the consultation process through appropriate techniques using photography and verbal commentary for them to reflect on their experience and express their views. The key was listening to children, not imposing an adult framework to which they had to respond.

The Patio Project opened in May 1993 on the Patio Estate, a small estate of 380 houses in Swinton, an ex-mining village on the northern edge of Rotherham. Four full-time staff were funded at the time by City Challenge and the project was managed by The Children's Society. The Society's work nationally is committed to work with young people to help fulfil their needs and rights. This includes developing a model of interaction with young people in the context of their neighbourhood on issues relating to how they use the environment.

Issues

Initially the project staff felt they were being viewed with great suspicion by people on the estate, who thought they were there to 'sort things out or put them right'. An informal 'drop-in' approach generated some response, which led to a small group of teenagers spending a weekend with the youth workers in Derbyshire, exploring what they felt about the estate and their lives on it. Various problems were discussed, particularly the fabric of the housing on the estate, such as black mould and damp in the dwellings, and the issue of how other people viewed the estate as trouble-torn and crime ridden. The teenagers felt that people thought they were poor because they wore cheap trainers and said that some young people were frightened to say that they lived there. The weekend evolved into a number of initiatives led by the young people themselves. One was a video project, another a visit to Wentworth MP Peter Hardy at the House of Commons, and another involved a more extensive survey of young people on the estate using the Priority Search technique, a computer-aided survey package (The Children's Society, 1995a).

Children's perceptions

Around the same time that the teenage consultation was getting underway, huge changes were also beginning to take place on the estate as part of a major refurbishment programme. The design and geography of the estate created a rare freedom of movement and this, alongside a building of trust between local people and the project, offered the project team a remarkable opportunity to work with very young children (three- to eight-year-olds) and consult them on their views of the neighbourhood. The team was aware of the adult-centred consultation exercise taking place at the time, through the Swinton Patio Community Survey, from which under-16s were excluded. Brian Wood, then project worker, commented 'the idea of consulting small children was a totally new concept to me ... Even with experience in consultation, it was a dramatic shift in thinking that allowed me to think and pursue ideas and mechanisms to consult them' (The Children's Society, 1994a).

The work started with a group of ten children discussing the advantages and disadvantages of their estate. The children held quite strong opinions on safety, play space, housing and the environment, and the project worker began to collect quotes from them on these issues. This led on to a tour of the estate with the children indicating places which were important, where they played and so on. The children were given the project's camera to take photographs of places which had particular significance for them. They conducted a running commentary as they went along – 'we're not supposed to go down there ... someone was murdered in that bush'.

This process was repeated three times, with the children leading the way and taking the photographs. 'What I had learnt from them was that they had strong views and opinions about their neighbourhood and also that they experienced it and used it in a very different way to older children and adults', the project worker said. The outcome of this exercise was a considerable amount of information in the form of photographs and quotes which were used to create a display. Additional work was generated in the form of different images of their neighbourhood and how places could be changed for the better.

The next stage was to consider ways of consulting with other children and the project worker worked with two groups of children to devise questions and agree on the process. Both groups came up with similar questions and when they met they were able to agree on the wording of the questions. For the project worker, the structure and use of language was a key issue: 'experience of this showed how children structure language differently to adults and communicate more effectively with each other ... [as an adult] they would tell me what they thought I wanted to hear, what they thought was the right answer ... it is a huge step forward to give them trust and control' (The Children's Society, 1994b).

The work from this project with children under eight has been written up into a report, *Children Should Be Heard* (The Children's Society, 1994b), and presented in a way which is also accessible to the children who participated in it.

The children involved presented the report to a group of local decision-makers and made proposals for changes that they would like to see during the refurbishment of the estate. The children were responsible for organising this event, the layout of the room and the way in which they presented their ideas.

Current developments

Since 1993, major changes have taken place on the estate. Everybody now has a garden, there are roadways for people to park their cars and the series of overhanging balconies, along with the car ports, have disappeared. The impact of these changes has been largely positive and has helped to transform the image of the estate. However, one 'safer by design' concept, where each roadway is a fenced-off cul-de-sac, has had a negative effect on children's mobility and freedom of movement, creating what has been described as 'children's reservations'.

The Patio Project team now operate from a base in Rotherham town centre as the Rotherham Participation Project, with a brief to work across the borough. During its residence on the Patio Estate, local children and young people continued their involvement through a number of different initiatives. A joint project between Patio Estate children and a Children's Society project in another ex-mining village in the same area involved some of those who had been involved in the consultation with the younger age group. The children from the Patio Estate were also invited to speak at the 1996 Community Links Conference in Leeds, where they talked about the two pieces of consultation and ran a workshop on strategies for consulting children.

Comment

A key concern in this project was to listen carefully to what children were saying rather than impose an adult framework to which they were invited to respond. In fact, children helped structure the research framework. Susan Francis, who was with the project from the beginning, commented on the benefits of this continued involvement:

> Over the three and a half years we were on the estate we had the opportunity to work with the same children from the age of three ... the children who were involved all the way shone out in terms of their confidence and ability to speak about their lives and were more able to state their own opinions rather than repeat those of their parents ... what we have learnt and what we hope to apply in our new borough-wide brief is to start earlier, before the decision-makers have made their choices, and to spend more time working with the decision-makers to enable them

to communicate with children and make that a meaningful and equal exchange. (Susan Francis, personal communication, 1996)

CASE STUDY 10	**Newbury Park School, Redbridge**	
	Role Play Exercise	Age 10–11

This project reports on a collaboration between a school and staff from a planning department. The planners acted as consultants to enable children to research a local development proposal and understand some of the complexities of the issues involved in redeveloping a site adjacent to the school.

Newbury Park Primary School is located in a heavily developed area in the London Borough of Redbridge. The school is bounded on three sides by land which is under a proposal for radical re-development, a site with a number of quite complex planning issues relating to different plots of the land. A large hospital, King George's, was recently moved from the site to a new location leaving two areas of land to develop, separated in part by the school playing field. The health authority involved in trying to dispose of the land had some interest from Sainsbury's for the development of a retail park. The local authority's response was that this was an inappropriate out-of-town location for a new shopping facility and decided to present its own ideas about how the area could be developed.

The Council wanted to see the area examined comprehensively. It was suggested that the school site should form part of the development area, with the intention of providing better facilities for the school and a more logical area of commercial development. Consultation had taken place with school governors and the headteacher, and an exhibition and consultation held locally attracted many parents. The school contacted the Planning Department for some detailed information about what was being proposed for the land around the school and from this came the idea of involving the students in considering some of the issues for themselves.

The result was a joint project, run by teaching staff and supported by staff from the Planning Department. Years 5 and 6 (140 children) were initially involved in some local area investigations. They walked around the immediate locality of the school, undertook some street surveys and did some observational surveys of the disused hospital, which is the key site in the development area. They also travelled a mile away to Barkingside and did surveys of the

LIVERPOOL
JOHN MOORES UNIVERSITY
AVRIL ROBARTS LRC
TEL: 0151 231 4022

use of the land around Barkingside High Street and particularly the pattern of retailing there.

The planning exercise itself was concentrated into a two-week period and there were two identical projects taking place in parallel with the Year 5 and 6 classes. Each class was divided into six working groups whose brief was to take on the role of various interest groups (local residents, the school, a retail developer, the health authority, the local Environmental Protection League and the local Council).

An initial presentation from one of the planners to the whole student group acted as a general introduction to what was happening in the local area, the role of the Planning Department and what a Public Inquiry is all about. Students then worked in groups, advised by a planner with school staff and parents, to develop their ideas. The residents' group, for example, had with it a member of the Planning Department as well as some parents and they discussed what residents might feel about the changes in the area and what they might want from the new development.

Following this input, the children were given a timetable of one week to prepare their suggestions for the site. They were assisted in this process with guidelines and key questions from the planners. The children had to prepare their proposals with a plan of the site and written evidence which was to be submitted to the Planning Department. During this week the groups were supported by their class teachers and parents. At the end of this first week the children's folders were sent to the Planning Department and they had a further week in which to complete their models and other visual aids for their presentation at a Planning Inquiry.

A few days before the Inquiry was held, the director of land managment who was to take the role of the inspector at the Inquiry, sent to the school questions for each group based on his reading of each proposal, which they would be asked at the presentation. The children were also informed that in addition to the three notified questions there would be two questions put to each group by the inspector on the day. They were asked to prepare some questions that they could put to the other interest groups involved in the presentation.

The final part of the Inquiry was set up in the school hall where each group made a ten-minute oral presentation to the director of land management and two planners who made up the inquiry team (see Figure 7). The children had also organised a small exhibition of their models and other drawings. After each group had made their presentation and answered their notified questions, they were then asked other questions and allowed a short time to discuss amongst themselves before responding. All six groups made their presentation and after each group the inspector made a summary of comments on their proposals.

Figure 7 Children at Newbury Park School proudly present proposals for developing their local neighbourhood to the director of land management. Photo courtesy of the *Ilford Recorder Newspaper*

The headteacher at the school described the project as a very challenging experience for the children. Firstly, they were involved in exercising their research skills. The Planning Department had provided a large amount of information that had been prepared for public consultation and these folders contained detailed information such as maps and data on existing planning proposals in the area. According to the headteacher, the project also demanded a high level of social interpersonal skills where pupils had to work in groups, discussing issues and making some crucial decisions, as well as organising their work. In his evaluation of the process, he commented that the group size of ten children trying to organise work was sometimes a little unwieldy. He felt they did an exceptional job in making key decisions and then allocating the work between them. The children also had to be aware of how others would view this process, which was something they were able to do fairly well, although they had not been exposed directly to the views of the various groups with interests in the site.

The audience at the presentations was very impressed by how logically and clearly children presented their arguments and ideas. One of the most interesting aspects was the challenge of responding to questions, particularly the unnotified questions. It was evident that the previous work had enabled them to think creatively and address the problems raised.

The children's project work and ideas, which included recreation provision and several pleas to include small cottage hospital facilities, were taken away by the team of planners who concluded the project by writing up an inspector's report. The planners felt they had benefited from hearing the children's ideas at first hand and discussing their proposals, which they considered to be feasible, realistic and thought-provoking. They found the experience both illuminating and enjoyable and were particularly impressed with how quickly the children picked up the difficult issues involved. For the headteacher, this project was a happy coincidence between the school's interest in learning about the local area and the Planning Department's initiative. His view was that the children were very enthusiastic about adults from outside paying careful attention to their ideas and taking them seriously.

Comment

This project illustrates the potential for exploring the complexities of development proposals with young people, as well as the way in which planners can act as consultants and advisers to help children develop their ideas and understand conflicts of interest in the local community. It was an exercise with a clear focus and structure provided by the planners involved and enabled young people to develop new insights into their immediate locality.

CASE STUDY 11	**Bradford**	
	Allerton Young People's Project	Age 10–18+

An estate regeneration initiative provided an important focus for this project. It highlights the energy and commitment which can be generated by a group of young people who have been encouraged to think and take action for themselves. It demonstrates the context in which this can happen and the partnerships which need to be established to support young people's efforts to realise their ideas.

Allerton Estate, four miles west of Bradford City Centre, was built during the 1940s and 1950s on farmland and then comprised 76 blocks of low-rise flats. Around 5300 people live in the area, including 730 young people aged 10–19 (1991 Census). The estate is described as an 'area of multiple stress, with high levels of unemployment, poor housing, racism, poverty and family breakdown'.

In May 1994, the Housing Department of Bradford Council launched a multi-million pound plan to regenerate the area. The Regeneration Strategy describes the objective of developing 'an Urban Village with a clear geographic and community identity...with good quality housing, a mix of tenures, opportunities for recreation and leisure, good quality social services and opportunities for employment and training' (Bradford City Council, 1994).

Since 1993, and as a result of funding from the Department for Education's Youth Action Programme, some innovative youth work initiatives have been developing on Allerton and two other nearby estates. Estate regeneration has provided a focus for the young people involved to consider their issues in relation to redevelopment.

Social action
The three-year government funding for these youth work schemes is linked to a crime prevention initiative, but the project workers involved were committed from the outset to working with young people using the social action model. This approach is used to enable young people to organise and take action on issues which they themselves identify. With a project already set up in Allerton running on traditional lines, the Centre for Social Action was asked to provide training for the new initiative and continued to provide support over the three years of the project.

In the early stages a housing group was established, as a result of concern about the lack of new property for single people. This evolved in February 1995, when workers at the project and the young people involved began a collaboration to research the needs of young people in the context of the Council's regeneration programme. The report published by the project explains 'the research was undertaken because of a commitment to making the views of young people heard. It is common for consultation processes and public meetings to be unattractive or inappropriate for young people to participate in, despite the good intentions of adults involved' (The Children's Society, 1995b).

Partnership

The preparation for the research evolved into a partnership between the Young People's Project, the City Centre Project, a housing advice service for young people on the estate and the MASTS Project, a supported housing scheme for young people in Allerton. The work involved in questionnaire design and a training programme for researchers was done by the partnership. However, during the summer of 1995, the City Centre Project on the estate was closed down, so the work was completed by the Young People's Project.

Methods

It was decided that two groups of people should undertake the questionnaires to reach the wide age range of young people on the estate. The City Centre Project worked with a group of over-16s and the Young People's Project recruited a group of 15-year-old students from Rhodesway School who lived on the estate. Training took place weekly in the school's tutorial sessions and was facilitated by the Young People's Project workers and someone who had left the school the previous year. The questionnaire was piloted at the school and the Young People's Project and a final version used to survey 300 people on and around the estate by ten trained interviewers from the two projects. The interviews were intentionally random, taking place during the day and evening within peer groups, on the streets and in school classes. The process took three weeks and 261 questionnaires were returned.

Young people's views

The report of the survey's findings states that 'the aim of the research was to find out the views of young people who hang about on the streets ... [and] are most likely to miss out on the conventional consultation processes'. Their findings indicated that 'young people have clear ideas of the type of youth facilities they want to see built on the estate'. They generally wanted to see a youth project on the estate rather than a youth club, which they saw as traditional centre-based youth provision, and in particular wanted facilities to be set up and run by the young people themselves. 'There should be a big sports centre run by young people. There should be coaches and youth work training for young people. Local youth workers are better. They know us and they know life on the estate.'

One group, 'Caz's Café Project', is an indication of the commitment to young people running their own project, 'not another case of adults asking us what we want and doing it all for us'. The group was formed at a time when discussions were underway on facilities for young people on the estate and the conclusion was reached there was 'nothing apart from the streets where the police were always moving young people on'. The group saw an opportunity to create their own space within the regeneration as well as something for all residents: 'We decided on a café rather than a youth club, because we want something for residents of all ages ... we are trying to break down the barriers between young and old'.

Consultation

A consultation process commenced in 1994. This involved looking at a number of options, consulting with local people, fundraising and considering a number of empty sites, as well as training and health and safety needs. An idea for a new building was developed and, with the help of an architect, the plans and ideas were displayed in the local regeneration office. Splits in the group emerged about a year and a half down the line, which the project workers helped the members involved to resolve. By October 1995, a stronger group emerged and various professionals were called upon to help plan strategy and establish a timetable. Between November 1995 and February 1996, a business plan was created and an application for Lottery funding submitted. During this time, two working groups were set up, each with a worker. These met several times a week under considerable pressure to meet the deadlines.

Conflict and compromise

A presentation was made at a neighbourhood forum where conflict arose with some residents about the proposed café in Lady Hill Park. After research and consultation, the group had decided on this as a suitable location for an informal meeting place for young people, both from the Allerton Estate and Allerton village. The residents started a petition against its location, which was countered with a petition by the project members. In March 1996, application for planning permission to go ahead with the development was submitted and in June a grant of £316,000 was awarded from the National Lottery Charities Board.

The plan, on the site of a former gardener's depot and disused public toilets, includes a function and games room, cafe and meeting room. The name, Caz's Café, is a dedication to the memory of Caroline Bacon who was heavily involved in the Café Project and who died of a stroke just after her sixteenth birthday. The café which the young people are to run will be overseen by a management committee of young people, parents, youth workers and other adults. The intention is to provide an information and advice service run by the recently organised peer education trainers. *The Young People's Project Review* (May 1996) concludes, 'we believe that other young people are going to respect Caz's Café because it was thought up and organised by young people and will inspire other young people to take action for themselves in a constructive way'.

CASE STUDY 12 **Shepherds Bush, London**
Godolphin Road Community Garden   Age 9–11

This case study highlights the benefits of young people's long-term involvement in a project relating to their locality. The work helped children understand the process of change and consider the quality of their local environment now and in the future. It gave them a new insight into and appreciation of a place which they had taken for granted.

The Godolphin Road community garden is situated in an area of high density housing in Shepherds Bush, west London. Before its development as a community garden, it was a derelict piece of land, the result of a bombing incident in the Second World War. In 1988, with the support and encouragement of Hammersmith and Fulham Council's Parks Department, the Godolphin Road Community Garden Association was set up with a committee of local residents. Their objective was to transform the site into a 'vibrant, lively garden ... a focal point for the whole area'. Some initial work had been undertaken by the Council and they provided a small grant to employ a coordinator for a few hours a week to deal with administration and the organization of volunteer work. Since that time, the Association's coordinator has been fundraising for resources to develop the site, mainly from charitable trusts and other sponsors of environmental improvements.

The garden is located in a part of the borough with very little open space, and for this reason is well used by residents, especially children. As the garden coordinator explained, 'Local children use this as their space, both in school time and in the evening. It's the one place in the area that they can meet in, otherwise it's a case of hanging around street corners'. Staff and students from the local primary school, Miles Coverdale, have been involved in the project from the outset, helping with maintenance and using the garden as a learning and teaching resource. The school has kept photographic and written records of the development of the site.

At the start of the project, the Council's Parks Department circulated a questionnaire to ask local people how they would like to see the garden develop. The most popular suggestion was the creation of a wildlife area and pond. Two years were spent building links with the local community and developing these two features and most of the work and maintenance was undertaken by local volunteers and school children. Work days, usually Sunday mornings, were organised and publicised at the school and regular visits were made to the garden during school time to talk to the coordinator, carry out gardening tasks, survey work, sketching and identifying plants. All of this helped to raise awareness in the school of the development process and, as the deputy headteacher suggested, to 'reinforce the site as their area and their environment ... you really get the sense that it's the children's pond because they built it. The outrage they express at the way people treat it ... for instance one boy brought in a number of mangled frogs in a box. They even use the garden as an excuse for being late because they've stopped to hike a trolley out of the pond'.

Ideas for the continued development of the garden were evolving through discussion within the Association. Local children had an involvement in the regular committee meetings and were able to comment on issues being raised. An overall plan was made for the development of the site, focusing on the need for disabled access to the area and the provision for formal and informal use by local children. It was recognised as important to build upon what had already been achieved by volunteers, particularly children, who had invested a considerable amount of time improving the area.

Through the Urban Programme, the Council provided funding for a feasibility study which was carried out by the Technical Planning Aid Service at Hammersmith and Fulham Urban Studies Centre. Consultation was carried out with the aim of involving as much of the local community as possible. The landscape architect from the Urban Studies Centre visited the school to discuss with the children their involvement with and use of the garden and to present ideas and possibilities to them through slides of other garden developments. Prior to this consultation exercise, plans of the garden had been displayed at the school showing stages of its development. A design exercise had been carried out with the children creating designs and making models of their ideas. According to the deputy headteacher, these had been completely unrealistic.

Following contact with school and other user groups to define needs, the landscape architect ran a design game with residents and school children at the Association's Annual General Meeting. A scale plan of the site was used with movable pieces to develop and illustrate the problems and potential of options. On the basis of the ideas generated, the landscape architect produced an initial sketch design for comments and criticism and finally a feasibility study, which was also displayed at the school. The feasibility study allowed for phased development as funds became available.

Development

The garden was closed down for the duration of the major works, but the school continued to make visits to the site to watch the heavy plant in operation, to take photographs to record the changes and to speculate on the way the site would look on completion. Basic landscaping started on site in September 1995, followed by turfing, seating and art work. An idea for a 'time capsule' was suggested during the excavations taking place on the site and the architect developed the idea of an hexagonal structure as a central feature of the new layout of pathways. Measuring approximately two feet high with a hollow centre of about a foot and a half across, the capsule was to be built with glass inserts at the top of it, so its contents could be viewed. The aim of the project was for children to generate material, both written and visual, which would be placed inside the time capsule structure and sealed (see Figure 8). Two local primary schools became involved in the project.

Time capsule

The idea for an educational project was developed around the theme of a time capsule for children to learn about how the area had changed since the turn of the century. It would enable them to express their views about those changes and articulate their hopes for how the area might change in the future. Various materials and activities were developed by the Urban Studies Centre around this past, present and future theme. A history trail of the locality using archive material, and particularly old photographs and extracts from old maps, helped the children develop a picture of change since the early 1900s. Their responses to these changes were mixed, but themes relating to play, traffic and safety predominated.

The children were involved in considering their quality of life in the area now, both good and bad features, and in developing their own indicators to assess environmental quality. Various activities took place relating to the environmental quality assessment, including traffic counts, scoring different features at different locations, and photography.

From all of this work, understanding what the area was like in the past and recording what it is like now, the children began to develop a picture of their hopes for life in the area in 2020, which is when the sealed capsule will be ceremoniously opened. They each wrote a short wish for how they hope life will have evolved: 'not so many cars and more bikes ... more flowers and more gardens ... no graffiti and no pollution and that people are nice to each other'. They were involved in presenting their ideas and their hopes, both at the official reopening of the community garden and at the launch of The Children's Society London programme aimed at encouraging young people to express their views about their locality.

Figure 8 Children from Miles Coverdale School make a contribution to the time capsule containing their visions for the future. Photo courtesy of *Hammersmith, Fulham and Shepherds Bush Gazette*

CASE STUDY 13 Craigmillar, Edinburgh EcoCity Age 7–11

This case study reports on a project supported by a range of local business and community groups. It emphasises the value of an interprofessional team of people working with children in an intensive way to develop their understanding of environmental change. It has enabled young people to contribute to the consultation process within a major regeneration programme.

EcoCity Projects

The EcoCity team from the Training, Advice, Support and Consultancy (TASC) Agency, Edinburgh, are training and education consultants, who are committed to involving children in decision-making which affects their lives and which creates a sense of involvement in their community. Their partners are architects and urban designers who work to enable communities to influence what happens to them. The EcoCity Projects began in 1992 during Britain's presidency of the European Community. In the initial projects, children worked to plan, design and build a scale model of their ideal 'environmentally friendly' city with the support of a multi-disciplinary team of architects, urban designers, artists, teachers and environmentalists.

Craigmillar

The EcoCity Project at Craigmillar, unlike the first two which created imaginary landscapes and cities, involved the development of a real location using a model based on a large-scale contour map. It was initiated as an opportunity for young people to contribute to the consultation process relating to a major regeneration programme in and around Craigmillar, Edinburgh. One of the significant changes taking place included a building development on the South East Wedge, a large, mainly green-field site adjacent to Craigmillar.

The Friends of Craigmillar, an Urban Aid funded project, were responsible for commissioning the EcoCity Project. They comprise 50 Edinburgh-based businesses and 40 Craigmillar community groups working in partnership on a range of projects to support the regeneration of the Craigmillar area, which has a much higher unemployment rate than the city average. In the context of the imminent development of the South East Wedge, and one of huge potential impact for the Craigmillar area, the Friends of Craigmillar wanted to create opportunities for children to participate in the community consultation process, as no mechanism had been put in place to achieve this.

Preparatory workshops

About three months before the project started, the EcoCity team comprising an architect, an urban designer and two members of the TASC agency, spent time in each of the four schools involved to introduce the project and run three preparatory workshops. The team wanted to ensure the children had enough background information to enable them to feel confident and knowledgeable when they came to the task of planning, designing and building their city. During the first workshop, the children were asked to consider the good and bad things about living in cities and to think of ten ideal features of the city. Stimulus material was available illustrating different kinds of energy sources and buildings around the world. This was also an opportunity for the team to pose questions and establish the children's current level of knowledge. In the second session, the children were introduced to the concept of working to scale, by assessing the size of furniture in the classroom in relation to the 1:200 scale EcoCity model. In the final preliminary session, the children were taken on a site visit to see the South East Wedge. They were able to view it and look out over Craigmillar from the top of Arthur's seat in the centre of Edinburgh. They also visited Dalkeith, a small town outside Edinburgh, to view different types of settlement, building decoration and street planning.

Five-day project

The next stage was for the children to work on a 20 by 20 foot model of the South East Wedge site at the local community centre for five full days to create their ideal Craigmillar of the future (see Figure 9). At the outset, the architect explained the contours of the model to the 40 children involved and orientated them, explaining the site and pointing out landmarks. It was considered important at the start to involve the group in something active, both for the children to get to know one another and for them to take ownership of the model. The group were asked to paint the model green, but to anticipate that this would be changed as the week progressed.

The urban designer then discussed with the group the next stage, 'the place making' part of the exercise, when they would need to describe what was going into their city. The children formed working groups of eight to discuss the previously generated material on the good and bad aspects of the city.

Each group of children had responsibility for developing two boards of the model within the context of the whole. Checking with neighbouring groups was essential so that each bit of the design related to the next. One of the support team had the role of helping the children come up with ideas and transferring

Figure 9 Children from Craigmillar in Edinburgh work on a large-scale model during an intensive five-day programme to plan an EcoCity. Photo: Scotsman Publications Ltd, Edinburgh

these on to the model in a way which linked in with the rest of the work going on. She questioned each group and challenged them to justify what they were doing.

Design ideas

The children designed a series of individual villages, each with their own identity, described by one of them as 'villages within a city – we've separated the villages by using water. We've built loads of bridges to go across it'. Another participant described the model:

> Four thousand people can live on the whole of our board. We've got businesses, we've got pensioners' houses, fields, vegetable farms. We've got everything ... primary schools, community areas, houses, police stations, fire stations, we've got EcoCity College, we've got leisure centres ... five or six windfarms and loads of solar panels. We don't have lots of roads because if there were more roads there would be more cars and more accidents. There's enough cars in Edinburgh as it is ... you can travel anywhere on this board on a tram.

Presentation

At the end of the week's work, the schools, parents, local politicians, public and private sector representatives, community workers and people involved in environmental education were invited to a presentation of the model. After the formalities, the group moved through to the area where the model was displayed, the lights went up and the children made their presentations. Each child then offered to show an adult around the model. One member of the TASC Agency described this as 'the point where the most impact is made, as adults begin to appreciate that the children actually understand and believe in what they've done'.

Evaluation

Following the EcoCity event, a workshop was held with local agencies, teachers, planners and developers to evaluate the process and outcomes. Participants commented on the children's success in producing a diverse spread of facilities and integrating these with a complex network of water, energy and transport links. Groups also commended the children's approach to the creation of separate 'villages' within the development, a key idea in their work which really differentiated it from the proposals put forward by the group of consultants who had made their own study and recommendations.

The range and status of the project backers reflected the seriousness with which the EcoCity Project was taken. The project team also considered that the real involvement of the private sector strengthened the impact of the project. It is hoped that the Craigmillar Project may be used as a basis and stimulus for involving more of the local community in the future of the South East Wedge.

Comment

A number of clear messages emerged from the EcoCity Project. The value of an interdisciplinary, interprofessional team, committed to developing children's understanding of environmental change, was evident in the way they enthused children and enabled them to engage in the design process. Because of the high ratio of adults to children, teachers were able to spend time discussing ideas and explaining concepts to children which is not always possible in the school situation. The partnership between the private sector, community groups and local schools demonstrated a very practical form of support for environmental education, extending what schools could manage to do for themselves.

It was possible in the preparatory workshops to extend children's experience and to establish certain understandings and skills. There was a different kind of value derived from the exciting and intensive week-long event, which provided an in-depth experience not always possible in schools because of the way the timetable is generally structured.

'EcoCity' implied not only an emphasis on green issues, but an interest in all kinds of relationships. Children understood that change to improve the quality of life would probably require changes in people's relationships with the environment, in the way transport systems might be organised, the generation and use of energy and the relationship between built form and natural form. They also learnt that every design decision has an impact on other elements and that there is a need to see the interrelationships between all aspects of a development. Above all, they had created a vision of the future which they could see and even touch. This had been presented as something exciting, positive and creative. The adults were shown convincingly that children were able to understand complex processes, and had contributed to the debate on the changing environment.

CHAPTER 10 Art, design and environment

This chapter focuses on the experience of young people who have been involved in environmental design projects. It describes the kinds of projects they tackled and the techniques they used. It hints at the ideas they explored and the problems they set themselves. It explains how they collaborated with professional designers and comments on the nature of their working relationship.

We are all potential designers, but will not develop our capabilities if we do not learn the appropriate skills. Young people can learn from a range of professionals in the fields of art, design and environment. Artists have helped young people make artworks to develop a sense of place or use graphic techniques to visualise future possibilities. Architects, landscape architects and ecologists are other professionals who have been able to involve young people in environmental design. Art and design institutions such as art schools and art galleries can contribute to education for participation. The key contribution here is the use of a visual/spatial language to explore ideas about relationships between structures, spaces and people, which is not possible through the medium of words alone.

In design projects, experiment and innovation are valued. Young people are encouraged to 'play' with ideas, try alternative possibilities, compare and contrast ways of thinking. The ideas are made visible and able to be shared. Young people are able to generate ideas, refine and develop proposals for change, and then through critique, select those solutions which are most appropriate for their purpose. Criticism is a very important part of the process. Through discussion and argument, comparing different possibilities, young people are able to make value judgements about quality. They are able to shape their thinking and articulate their ideas. They learn ways to communicate their ideas, develop an argument and persuade others – all important skills in participation.

The difficulty is in deciding on the complexity or depth of study required for a particular project. There is danger that judgements can be made on the basis of inadequate information or decisions made without a thorough analysis of the problem. Sometimes, when individual group members tackle different aspects of a design project, they do not have a clear idea of how all the component parts fit together; the key is to be able to make links and connections between ideas. Working in groups to develop critical skills or design capability makes a different set of demands, requiring social and interpersonal skills to encourage everyone to contribute.

CASE STUDY 14 **Urban Studies Centre, London Thames Path Guide** Age 9–11

Hammersmith and Fulham Council has a commitment to enhancing the quality of the riverside environment and the maintenance of a riverside path. The project enabled the children involved to understand and appreciate their environment and develop an enhanced sense of place. They were able to publish a guide to the area, something of lasting value for the local community.

The Thames Path, which follows the River Thames for 180 miles from its source in Gloucestershire to the Thames Barrier in London, is now a Countryside Commission National Trail, described as the only long-distance walking route to follow a major river.

During 1995, a partnership project was developed between the Countryside Commission, Hammersmith and Fulham Urban Studies Centre and United Distillers. The Countryside Commission wanted to raise the profile of their newest National Trail and initiate projects which would encourage people to walk the Thames Path and explore its features.

An approach was made to the Hammersmith and Fulham Urban Studies Centre to involve them in an educational project which would raise awareness of the riverside environment in the local community. The Urban Studies Centre is an educational charity and resource base for learning about the local area funded by Hammersmith and Fulham Council. It has extensive experience of developing projects with schools focusing on the six-mile stretch of riverside in the borough, particularly in relation to the uniqueness of the riverside environment and its contribution to quality of life. A proposal was developed by the Urban Studies Centre to work with a number of local schools on a project which would lead to the young people involved producing information and material for a guide to the area. United Distillers, whose head office is in

Hammersmith, offered sponsorship funding for the project and the printing of the guide, which was to be produced and made available free of charge to the local community.

Figure 10 A pupil researches riverside history to prepare a guide on the Thames Path in Hammersmith and Fulham

The Urban Studies Centre worked with six primary schools during the summer of 1995 and helped them to explore the section of the path nearest their school. The students were engaged in a range of activities and themes focusing on the historic, economic, social and environmental importance of the Thames. They visited the foreshore to discover the ecology and wildlife of the river, explored historic landmarks and riverside buildings and architecture, learnt about the working waterfront as it was and as it is today and how the area is evolving for the future (see Figure 10). As with all of the work of the Urban

Studies Centre, this project was aimed at increasing young people's understanding and appreciation of their locality and how it changes. This process was enhanced through the participation of a range of groups and local people in projects; particularly successful during this one was the contact with elderly people who talked about changes they had witnessed along the riverside.

The material generated by the young people on a range of themes was used to produce the guide. The result is an attractive and illuminating collection of pieces of factual writing, poetry, observational studies, oral history reminiscence, personal accounts as well as drawing and art work, all linked to a map and guided walk along the Thames Path. Copies of the guide were distributed widely through libraries, leisure centres and similar outlets in the borough.

Children and young people have an enormous enthusiasm for learning about where they live and in their evaluation of this project expressed the real pleasure they experienced exploring a relatively familiar place, making contact with different people and learning from a range of sources: 'I was amazed how much I didn't know'; 'We got to learn things from outside the school'; 'I liked going to see the pensioners and I liked talking to them'.

Comment
Projects like this which focus on developing a sense of place are able to build on children's local and personal experience and develop skills and knowledge which are both important and transferable. It is an opportunity for the local authority to present positive images of the borough and to publicly value children's perceptions.

CASE STUDY 15 **Cambridge City Council
Refurbishment of Recreation Areas**   Age 5–14

Collaboration between two council departments enabled children and young people to feed ideas into the design process for the renovation of two play and recreation areas in Cambridge. They were able to make their views known to the landscape architect responsible for the scheme through a series of community arts initiatives and a design day for adults and children held at the local community centre.

The idea to involve young people in a community design exercise came from officers at Cambridge City Council. The Council had been unhappy about previous consultation initiatives, and wanted to engage both children and adults in an exercise which would create a real understanding of the issues of urban regeneration. It was decided to organise a community design day, with opportunities to include children in the design process, as they were prime users of the two recreation areas under consideration.

Planning and preparation

The team which planned and carried out the consultation programme included officers from the Departments of Community Development, Play and Community Arts. A freelance consultant acted as facilitator and led meetings to discuss plans and ways of working with the community. A site visit was arranged to consider how best to organise the community design day. A half-day training session was held for the council officers and community artists who would be involved in the event. Although many had experience of working with children and young people, none had specific skills in facilitating participation in the design process. Students from Anglia Polytechnic University were also invited to act as facilitators at the community design day.

Community arts workshops

Local schools did not respond enthusiastically to the invitation to participate because of other pressures on the curriculum and changes in staffing. Instead, the community arts centre organised half-term sessions on photography to explore the subject of children at play and outdoor recreation. Small groups of children made a photographic record of visits to places where children play, outdoor interactions between children and adults, people and their activities in the recreation ground, landscape features, secret places, and child-friendly places. Those supporting them used the opportunity to talk to adults and children about play issues.

Community design day

The community design day was held at Ross Street Community Centre, with the planning team, the landscape architect responsible for the landscape renovation, community artists, play and youth workers and two geography students. A key contributor was a resident who had been involved in the planning meetings and had worked directly with local children to interest them in the project. Around 30 residents, men and women, spanning a wide age range, contributed to the day (see Figure 11). Special interest groups such as disabled people were represented. Younger children under ten years old, accompanied by adults, and some 14-year-olds also participated.

Figure 11 Young people and adult residents of Ross Street discuss plans for the refurbishment of two local recreation areas in Cambridge with the landscape architect responsible for the scheme

In the central hall, an exhibition of photographs with comments from children on play activities and play spaces was displayed and there was space to pin up work in progress. A simple model representing the recreation areas had been produced. Materials were provided, such as card, coloured papers, pens, adhesive and scissors. Multiple photocopies of photographs of the site were available. A community design pack had been prepared to create a framework for thinking and provided an easy reference and aide memoire for ideas for site appraisal and a stimulus for generating ideas for change.

After a brief introduction, working groups were established and their first task was to make a site visit for an appraisal of the existing situation. This was followed by problem identification, where the residents marked elements requiring change on large-scale maps. They were very aware of the problems and inadequacies of the existing site and were able to articulate them readily.

The next stage was more challenging – how to generate ideas for change and to consider a variety of options. Where adults had been content to discuss problems without coming up with any solutions, the children showed the value of a visual language for thinking about change. They had found it difficult to break into adult discussions, but had understood the issues being debated. The facilitator encouraged them to extricate themselves from the groups and sort out some ideas through the use of visual media. Through experimenting with annotated sketches and photomontage, they were able to identify a range of alternative possibilities. Not only did they have ideas for improvements, but they were more ready than adults to express these and share them with others. The adults rushed to incorporate their ideas in the groups' proposals.

Sketches, photomontages and notes were pinned onto annotated maps, which began to show very convincingly the range of issues and ideas which groups were exploring. These stimulated further discussion, focusing on the experiences and activities which play and recreation spaces should provide for and what the design implications might be. Animated discussion continued through the lunchtime and into the afternoon, when various options for change were hotly debated. A collection of slides of other children's environments and landscape examples was seen by some members of the working groups who fed ideas back to their colleagues. By the end of the afternoon, groups had taken their ideas as far as they could and were ready to make presentations. A positive attitude to critique encouraged others to respond, question and comment and a general consensus emerged. Interestingly, the demand was not for new facilities and play equipment. What was wanted was an overall improvement in quality of landscaping such as planting, to give varied ground cover, provide screening and divide the space, and to create a particular sense of place. The discussion then moved away from design issues to implications for management and maintenance.

Evaluation

The landscape architect found enormous value in being able to talk directly with adults and young people about their needs and desires. She felt that designers should meet users if they are to produce anything relevant. The residents appreciated the experience of meeting council officers face to face in a collaborative setting, and said they were now aware that problems of renovating recreational spaces were more complex than they had first imagined. The children enjoyed the experience of working with adults and being able to make a useful contribution. They were proud that their drawings had not been used just as an afterthought to the main business of the meeting, but had made a significant contribution to developing ideas for change. Council officers were content that the day had established an approach to consultation which resulted in a much clearer idea of residents' needs and wishes.

CASE STUDY 16   **Salford City Council**
Islington Park Renovation Project   Age 3–11

These two projects illustrate a successful collaboration between Salford City Council's Technical Services, the Arts and Leisure Department, a school and community artists. Children generated ideas which were developed by the artists to transform the local environment. The Council's commitment to public art was a means to develop a sense of place and a greater degree of community involvement, resulting in a reduction in vandalism.

Islington is an area which is part of the old centre of Salford, Greater Manchester. The Islington Park Scheme was initiated in spring 1990 as part of Salford City Council's five-year commitment to a programme of renewal for the Islington Estate, a run-down area of council housing and commercial properties. For the headteacher of St Philips Primary School, Salford, collaboration with Salford City Council on environmental improvement projects has been 'an important part of a package; it very much complements the way we work inside the school and that is to try to raise everybody's expectations and aspirations'. The school took part in two initiatives – firstly to contribute to the development of a new community park in Islington, an area near the school, and more recently to regenerate the school's grounds.

The site under initial consideration, bordering the Islington Estate, was a disused and vandalised former Methodist mission hall and burial ground, which was not suitable for building on because of its former use as a mass grave. In the mid-1950s the surrounding area was redeveloped for residential use, with three-storey blocks of flats and two tower blocks. The gravestones were removed and the site received some basic landscaping during the 1960s; it was subsequently vandalised.

A scheme to create an attractive and useful park area was proposed. In communications between City Technical Services Department and the Arts and Leisure Departments, it was decided that art could play an important role in developing the character and community significance of Islington Park and there would be significant benefit in developing artwork in collaboration with the local community.

Following public consultation, ideas generated by local people on the estate were incorporated in design proposals for a new community park drawn up by landscape designers in the City Council's Technical Services Department. Community artists, Chrysalis Arts, were commissioned to develop the work, with a brief to oversee that maximum community involvement was maintained at all times in the design and development of artwork proposals.

The working party of the Council's Art Officer, Landscape Designer and Chrysalis Arts took an early decision that the artwork should be incorporated into the permanent infrastructure of the park. Chrysalis prepared formal proposals for the key features of the site – ornamental gates, a central mosaic and seating. Their design and development were discussed at a series of workshops with local people.

Chrysalis Arts organised a 16-day residency at St Philips Primary School to work with children on the mosaic design. The thematic content of the mosaic, representing different aspects of local life, was developed by the teachers and artists. Children worked with ceramic shards donated to the school by a local manufacturer, to create images for the different themes of the mosaic. A classroom area was closed off and a concrete mixer brought in. Chrysalis Arts worked with the children and members of the local community breaking the ceramic tiles, creating designs and mixing concrete in which to set the 101 panels of the mosaic. Each design was cemented into a concrete mould ready for laying in the middle of a seating area in the centre of the park.

The gates and seats were designed with the involvement of a range of local groups and individuals, including the local youth club and a group of senior citizens. Initial ideas were tried out on paper before full-scale designs based on different themes were put together on cardboard. These designs were then used and translated into steel by blacksmiths in the Council's Art and Leisure Department. Following final installation of the work, the park was opened by local children at a celebratory event in August 1991. This included a parade through the estate, a picnic in the park, a brass band playing and additional temporary artworks.

For the City of Salford planners, the most important aspects of the scheme were its inter-departmental approach to renewal and the opportunity for the input and involvement of local people. For Chrysalis Arts, the project was 'successful in achieving its community involvement and in generating a sense of ownership and pride ... in the short term at least'. They highlighted other considerations such as additional time demands, the need to relinquish an element of design control and the risk of complications with the main contractor on site, but felt that these were more than offset by the creation of an urban landscape of cultural significance and meaning to its users.

Comment

Additional opportunities might have been created in this partnership for young people to learn about the role of the different council departments in local decision-making through direct contact with officers. It would also have been valuable for them to have seen how artists and craftsmen – the blacksmith, for instance – interpreted and translated their ideas into finished art works.

One opportunity, that of further participation in environmental renewal, was taken up however, with a project to improve the boundary and playground areas of St Philips. The school's chainlink boundary fence was damaged, its play spaces poorly designed and its grass and planted areas worn out. On the basis of the success of the Islington Park project, planners at Salford City Council again acted as coordinators to bring together the city's landscape architects, the school and Chrysalis Arts to participate in improvements to the school grounds.

Chrysalis Arts spent a week in the school beforehand in order to get a feel for school life. The artists then spent two weeks working in the school with children, parents and staff. Design ideas depicting the history of the school and its activities evolved from the workshops and were used for the final design of the boundary railings. The children's drawings and computer designs were recreated in steel and enamelled plates. One pupil has a permanent place there. She explained, 'One day I was doing a cartwheel in PE and the people who helped us with the fence took a photograph of me. It was used to make a metal figure of a girl which is fixed in the railings. I'm very proud that I will be in the fence for ever and ever'. The railings are ingeniously fanned which gives the impression of movement.

Other features which the children suggested and designed included railing heads, brass busts representing staff at the school and people from the local area. Chrysalis cast these from papier mache models made by the children. The headteacher commented, 'The staff had reservations, but we didn't interfere. I'm on the corner looking like Napoleon, but three years later everything is still intact'.

The scheme, completed in June 1993, received funding from the Urban Programme and North West Arts. A representative from Salford City Council said, 'This scheme is perhaps a pointer to what life and planning should really be all about – helping people to shape their environment and to take a stake and pride in its future'. And the final word from the headteacher 'It isn't something we've stood still on. We've now moved forward on putting games on the ground, all done in consultation with the children. The children have raised the money to have the games painted themselves'.

CASE STUDY 17	**Royal Academy of Arts, London**	
	Living Bridges Exhibition	Age 16–17

An exhibition of designs for bridges provided an exciting stimulus for workshops organised through a partnership between an educator and an architect. These were used as a springboard for design studies in schools and colleges.

The end of the century and the beginning of a new millennium inevitably creates anticipation of a new era. Questions concerning how we choose to live, what the environment will be like, and the implications for design and technology are in our minds. How might young people be involved in the debate about the shape of things to come? This was a question considered by the Education Department at the Royal Academy of Arts in a workshop programme set up for students visiting the 'Living Bridges' exhibition. A series of eight day-long workshops was organised by the Education Department, designed for different groups of 16- to 17-year-old students involved in Art and Design Technology NVQ and GNVQ courses and Art and Design 'A' level. The facilitators were a research fellow from the Division of Education at South Bank University and an architect at Kingston University, who worked with the students and their teachers from schools and colleges as far away as Manchester and Devon as well as London, Surrey and Essex. Students were expected to do preparatory work beforehand, exploring ideas about people, place and the notion of 'habitation'. The workshop introduced them to ideas and methods involved in environmental design.

Brief

Students were invited to respond to a competition brief for a new pedestrian bridge across the River Thames. They were advised that it should not be designed in isolation from its surrounding urban environment, and one of the principle concerns should be to reduce the divisive nature of the Thames. Alternative transport systems should be considered and the issue of access for people with impeded mobility addressed. The workshop focused on relationships between the site, the people who use the new bridge, the ways in which the bridge might function, its structure and appearance.

Figure 12 Students in a design workshop at the Royal Academy of Arts discuss with an architect their proposals for a new bridge across the Thames

Opportunities and constraints

Working in groups, students thought how their proposal might impact on the existing site, and whether or not it would create a complementary or contrasting feature in terms of scale, form or the use of materials. They discussed the different needs of the office workers, tourists and theatre-goers, who would be the principle users of the bridge. They debated the functions the bridge might serve, not merely as a link between two sides of the river, but as a location for work, commerce, entertainment, leisure and sight-seeing. They explored the merits of basic bridge structures, such as arch, truss, cantilever and suspension and considered which might be appropriate for use on this particular site and what materials might be suitable (see Figure 12).

Exhibition

The dramatic installation of the exhibition, where the models were set above a 'river' of water, surrounded by drawings, photographs and plans, created an exciting focus for research. Students responded well, finding much to interest them, including the design content and techniques in model making and presentation. The exhibition provided a wonderful source of ideas and an opportunity for students to analyse and appraise the work of other designers before embarking on their own design project.

Design activity

Study activities focused on techniques for thinking, analysing, criticising and designing. Groups involved students from different schools, with different levels of ability and experience. One exercise was to produce maps of the site, identifying key features. There was a variety of responses, including drawing, paper collage and 3-D presentations. Another exercise was to brainstorm ideas for a new bridge and to formulate sketch possibilities. Time was spent in generating ideas, discussing them, arguing, drawing, comparing notes, more arguing, considering alternatives, more arguing, developing ideas through collaborative working and presenting their work.

In carrying out the design project, students were advised of the need to formulate questions as a focus for their investigations and explorations. These concentrated on the requirements of the client, the needs of the users, the functions the bridge would serve, as well as the opportunities and constraints offered by different materials and forms of construction. Students had to think not only about the content of their designs, but how they might share their ideas with others. In the workshops, they used annotated sketches and diagrams, collage and simple card models, but at college they would be able to use different kinds of drawings and plans, photomontage and more complex models to develop their thinking and present the results of their work. It was suggested their presentation should include:

- an analysis and interpretation of the existing site

- a plan of their design for a new bridge, showing how it related to the context and works as an inhabited space

- a section explaining the main spatial ideas and the way the bridge related to the river, the banks and beyond

- a series of images to suggest the impact of the new bridge on the riverscape

Comment

Students were able to explore complicated design issues inspired by the work of architects and engineers. Some students' designs showed ingenuity and originality, incorporating ideas for parks and water treatment centres in the bridge design, while others stuck with the familiar idea of the shopping mall and sports centre. Some students were concerned with ecological concepts, others emphasised more social and cultural concerns. Teachers felt that the students had benefited from the concentrated experience: they had been greatly stimulated by the exhibition material, and had been exposed to new ideas and vocabulary through discussion and debate. They had learnt more about the nature of design through the process of questioning, hypothesising, generating and testing ideas, and were now more confident to tackle design projects and to critique the work of others.

CHAPTER 11 # School grounds

The school is the most obvious starting point for children and young people to look again at a familiar environment and consider possibilities for improvement. The development of school grounds presents wonderful opportunities for young people not only to be involved in conceptualising ideas for change, but in many cases, to actually see their ideas realised.

Projects to develop school grounds are widespread in the UK. These bring both environmental and educational benefits. In many instances, children contribute to the thinking about change and sometimes help to put their ideas into practice. Teachers cannot engage the children in a full experience of design because their own training does not necessarily address this area, so there is a need for a working partnership with individuals or agencies who can offer design expertise. The support of designers can not only result in a better quality environment but can also extend educational opportunities for children, both in using the new environment and by participating in the design process. Through this experience, children are more likely to value the changes, and care for their environment. The particular value of developments in school grounds is that these are very familiar environments which children know intimately and which have great significance for them.

Projects need to focus on the use of the environment as an educational resource. Cosmetic change may result in neglect. From their work in school grounds, children learn that every design decision has not only a cost implication, but a maintenance implication, so they begin to understand the close relationship between design, development and management of an environment.

There are often problems of timing. Children want change to happen quickly and are sometimes disheartened at the amount of time it takes for even relatively small changes to take place. This points to the need for phased development, where children can see things happening, but developments do not have to be rushed when costly mistakes can be made. It also gives children time to monitor the impact of the changes and learn that change is not always desirable in itself, as it may not necessarily solve problems, just create new ones.

CASE STUDY 18   **Gillespie School, London**
Islington Schools Environment Project   Age 9–10

The project to design playground markings at Gillespie School was the result of interprofessional collaboration between a teacher and an artist. Children were enabled to visualise and test out possibilities for change through various modelling techniques in an effort to improve the play quality of their school grounds.

Involving children in an experience of environmental design has been a feature of the work at Gillespie Primary School for a number of years. Their work has been inspired by the director of the Islington Schools Environment Project (ISEP), an artist who helped shape this project as part of a series of design education initiatives in the school.

In terms of children's participation at Gillespie School, there were three key aspects to the work: involvement in the process of environmental design as part of the school curriculum; contributing to environmental improvement; and working with an outside agency. The project involved a class of nine-year-olds and their teacher, and was initiated by a concern to improve opportunities for play. The structures designed by previous groups of children working with artists had been so successful that they had created a 'honeypot' effect: children crowded round them and neglected other spaces. The teacher wanted to create opportunities for collaborative group work and a chance for the children to develop higher self-esteem. She was anxious that the project should not be additional to their usual work, but could be incorporated within the requirements of the National Curriculum. In fact, all subjects were brought into play during the research phase, though art, design and technology and language were perhaps the most significant.

Preparation
The teacher planned a cross-curricular programme of work on the topic of games. This included consideration of sports, leisure activities, ball games and other outdoor games. Games from other countries were tried out. Parents and other adults were interviewed to find out about the games they used to play. It stimulated discussion on the needs of different age children and the prefer-

ences of boys and girls as well as work on bullying. In the design work, children were able to explore ideas about the nature of play. As a stimulus, the artist presented them with a slide programme of previous work.

Appraisal

As well as exploring the nature of play, the children set about exploring the playground. The idea was to look afresh at a familiar environment and consider its potential for change and improvement. Their first task was to identify places from the collection of cropped photographs which the artist had taken of the site. This proved difficult until the children went outside to search for things they had glimpsed. They discovered many things they had not noticed before. The next task was to map the site and identify where children chose to play and what games they played. Trundle wheels were brought into play for the measurements, and clipboards and questionnaires gave an official air to the children carrying out the play surveys (see Figure 13). When the results were analysed, it was evident that large areas of the playground were not used.

Figure 13 Pupils at Gillespie Primary School in Islington carry out surveys to investigate play activities in the school playground

When thinking about games which would make good use of the large space, the idea of markings for the playground was suggested. The children discussed the use of signs and symbols to control movement, such as traffic and directional signs and symbols at airports. A study of catalogues of commercially produced markings provided opportunities for critical appraisal, which extended their vocabulary and gave them some practice not only in making judgements, but in being prepared to explain and justify their preferences and choices.

Design activity

Having identified the need for change and done some research, the children were uncertain how to continue. The artist suggested they stop work on their design project and play with some things he had brought in – a collection of coloured metal washers, a bag of leaves, a collection of books on mazes. As they played with the shapes, looked at the patterns and read the stories, they began to think up ideas for playing games in the playground. Each child presented their idea for a new game to the group, then each group chose one and worked on it cooperatively.

Play supervisors advised on safety aspects and explained about movement within and through a space. They told the children that the positioning of the markings would be important: not too near structures, doors or in the football area. They suggested that they should be flexible and adapt to a variety of games, so that there would be something for all the children to play. The children incorporated their ideas into their plans and developed their ideas further. Proposals from each group were considered by the whole class and the 'underwater maze' was chosen as the final design. From this, the artist designed a drawing from which the painters could work.

Realisation

The markings were chalked out and the pupils tested them through playing a variety of jumping, hopping and 'chase' games. Some of the shapes were modified in response to advice from the children and to avoid drains and cracks in the tarmac surface. It was important that the markings did not cause any safety problems. The Friends of Gillespie funded the painting of the markings. The class carried out an evaluation of their work by monitoring how the markings were used.

Viewpoints

The teacher welcomed the partnership with the artist and felt able to extend her professional skills. She acted as an interpreter and facilitator when she felt it was difficult for the children to understand, and set a secure framework of expectations and behaviour. The artist established a link with the world outside school which helped the children see the relevance of their learning to real situations. The pupils were enthusiastic about the value of group work, explaining that it helped them get things done a lot quicker, but that they had to learn to explain ideas and not at the wrong time. The headteacher stressed the view that environmental change was part of the real world and part of children's lives: 'When their work is seen in public, it takes on another meaning for them, it becomes real. Their motivation, commitment and quality of work improve. This approach to education is about children's autonomy and empowerment, their ability to make democratic decisions'.

Comment

The project gave pupils a fresh awareness of their school environment, helped them to become more aware of play issues and enabled them to contribute to environmental improvement. There were opportunities for both independent and group work. The learning was purposeful, with a clear outcome. The children had to use language in a variety of situations, questioning other children about their play activities, critiquing commercial practice, brainstorming ideas in a group, discussing play issues with adults, explaining a complex set of rules for a new game and persuading colleagues to accept their ideas. Mathematics were involved in measurements and scale, in analysing and presenting information on play activities and games preferences. Art was used as a way of recording the environment, generating and presenting ideas for change. The pupils understood that design is not necessarily getting what you want, but finding something that will satisfy the needs of a wider group and will probably be the result of experiment, negotiation and compromise. Their efforts resulted in improved play facilities which benefited all pupils. The teacher's knowledge of the children and the artist's knowledge of the design process meant that they were guided through the various stages of the work to achieve a result which had both educational and environmental value.

CASE STUDY 19	**Durand Primary School**	
	Community Design for Gwent	Age 7–11

This report describes the work of a community design agency working in collaboration with a primary school. It shows how children are able to work with adults to engage in the design process. It demonstrates the importance of children doing thorough research before they develop proposals for change and emphasises the value of their organising own consultation programmes.

Community Design for Gwent

Community Design for Gwent Group, based in Newport, was established in 1985 with funding from the Urban Programme. It was set up to provide a range of design and technical services on a grant-aided basis to schools, community and voluntary groups, with the broad aim of maximising community involvement in the design and planning process. An education officer works with schools and communities to increase the level of consultation and participation in practical environmental projects.

Work with schools

School grounds are under-developed and under-used as an educational resource. However, research has suggested that the better the quality of the school landscape, the more it will be used and enjoyed, providing an improved educational experience. Although pupils and teachers are not short of ideas for making improvements, they are often unsure about how to put their ideas into practice. Too often, they start out with a list of what they want in terms of ponds, seats and hedgerows without asking the fundamental questions of why the site should be improved and who will benefit. There is perhaps an assumption that any change will be beneficial, particularly on sites with unfriendly and unpleasant conditions. Changing the school site is a complex process and requires good organisational skills as well as an understanding of the educational opportunities which can be developed. To be successful, the work in schools grounds should be directly related to the school curriculum and should address the following:

- the organic nature of site improvement projects

- the importance of carrying out surveys and appraisal

- the commitment of the whole school

- involvement of outside agencies

- roles and relationships (pupil, teachers, parents, designer)

- cross-curricular learning

- participation in processes of consultation, design and implementation

- action plans (curriculum development and management)

Durand School

Durand Primary, Junior and Infants School in Caldicot is a single-storey 1970s building set in a large, flat and exposed site. There are two tarmac playgrounds and the rest of the site is grassed. A busy main road passes the school, which is bounded by chainlink fencing and single trees. Access to the school is through a staff car park which borders the infants' playground. Teachers had been trying to make improvements for 15 years, but with little success.

The headteacher decided that an overall plan was needed and invited Community Design for Gwent to carry out a study of the nature and quality of the children's play and the problems which teachers and supervisors faced. The survey was carried out by an environmental science student on placement and pupils were involved in the research activity, which took one month. Games tended to be in single-sex groups. Play activities included boys playing football and girls involved in different types of 'chase' games. A large number of children were involved in little or no physical activity, passing the time sitting, standing and watching others or talking to friends. There was also some imaginative play, with infants pretending to be trains or ponies. Many children felt that playtime was 'boring' with 'not enough to do'. The next step was to try out various strategies to influence children's behaviour and monitor the effect of the changes. Pupils were invited to reflect on the behaviour patterns and assess the changes and to suggest their own ideas for improving playtimes.

The pupils' choice of the top ten things that were good in the playground included: 'plenty of room when allowed on the grass, the grass, playing "semi to semi", shelters, trees, square in the corner of the junior playground, lines, different kinds of spaces, playing hopscotch, variety of games'. Those things they liked least included: 'nothing to do, boys playing football, bareness and plainness of the playground, hard surface, muddy patches, not playing on the grass when it is wet, not enough room on the yard, only allowed on part of the grass, bigger boys bullying, no hopscotch lines'. The favourite games were 'semi to semi, ball games, line games, bulldogs and catch'. Other preferred activities were 'running around, TV programmes, polo and talking'.

Project development

The next stage was to formulate proposals to improve the playground. This involved an exploratory stage, where pupils and teachers considered the advantages and disadvantages of the play spaces. They learnt traditional and new playground games, tested out a variety of 'playkits' and different kinds of play equipment and experimented with some temporary low-cost play features. The research was developed over a long period. Feedback was sought through questionnaires devised by pupils, teachers and lunchtime supervisors and the research was carried out by the Friends of the Playground, a group of pupils who represented the others in the discussions on design and development.

The next planning stage involved design sessions. Community Design for Gwent identified environmental considerations and drew attention to site conditions and possibilities for improved facilities. Teachers contributed ideas for curriculum activities and children were able to draw on their experience of play. Parents and lunchtime supervisors were also invited to contribute. Whereas pupils were concerned with concepts such as spatial freedom, the ability to explore and take ownership of spaces, teachers were more concerned with problems of supervision and safety. Ideas were recorded on large-scale maps and models and an exhibition of ideas prepared for parents and design and environmental professionals to discuss schemes with pupils. Pupils and staff voted for their preferred scheme.

Design

The next stage was for Community Design for Gwent to produce a sketch scheme with costings and construction implications. When the school had accepted this, the final scheme was produced and a development plan agreed. Ideas to be incorporated include number squares, metre squares, 100-metre markings, hopscotch markings, covered sandpits, water features, sheltered areas against wind, screens against traffic noise, weather station, seating, terracing, amphitheatre, small gardens, raised planters, litter bins with lids and textured surfaces. The aim was to accommodate the design proposals developed through the research and consultation while providing for change, flexibility and growth. Target areas were identified for a five-year development programme. A management committee involving pupils, teachers and outside agencies is monitoring development.

Comment

Pupils were involved at all stages of the development, carrying out the initial research, discussing the need for change, helping to formulate and test out initial proposals and to develop ideas for the final design. The strategy of involving them in research activity helped them to identify the issues involved and address the question of why changes should be instituted. Testing out different kinds of play equipment demonstrated that design solutions are not always the most appropriate to improve quality of environmental experience; sometimes change in how activities are managed is more effective. Techniques of engaging children in the design process helped them to understand the different needs and values of the various people who would be affected by their proposals. This means that the changes are more likely to succeed, as the children will understand the thinking behind them. Their involvement will continue as new developments are monitored. Also, phased development with specific targets each year means that the children's interest will be sustained. The overall design means that development will be coherent rather than piecemeal.

| CASE STUDY 20 | **Newcastle Architecture Workshop City Challenge Schools Project** | Age 7–11 |

This case study reports on a project funded by City Challenge to improve the grounds of 12 primary schools. The support of a multi-disciplinary team of designers and teachers and the availability of funding meant that children's ideas were realised and environmental improvements put into effect. The report explains the design and educational processes involved.

City Challenge

The impetus for setting up the Environmental Improvements to School Grounds Scheme within the City Challenge Environmental Improvement initiative came from the Leisure Services Department of Newcastle City Council. It was designed to involve children and their parents in environmental improvements, by developing school grounds as a community resource. Officers realised that environmental improvements within the neighbourhood would not survive unless residents developed a sense of ownership over the schemes. Newcastle Architecture Workshop's aim was to give young adults and children an experience of active citizenship and demonstrate that they could influence and determine change in their environment.

The project was part of a rolling programme from 1991 to 1997 within City Challenge. The Newcastle Architecture Workshop worked with each school, both during the design phase and implementation phases. They supported schools' efforts in curriculum development, facilitated community development and offered technical aid and advice.

Curriculum development

The project commenced with in-service training for school staff to develop their understanding of the project, enable them to integrate it into their curriculum planning and to contribute to the design brief for the development of the school grounds. Following this, the teachers worked with the education officer from the Newcastle Architecture Workshop to plan the projects in each school. In each school, one class or year group was chosen as the design team. The programme of work, which was reviewed each week, was flexible, reflected the needs of individual schools and was adapted for different ages.

Design process

The development of the work followed certain stages for which the Newcastle Architecture Workshop devised appropriate techniques. The first was to raise children's awareness of the environment and develop a sense of place. They investigated the site in order to view it with fresh eyes. Techniques developed by the Workshop such as 'sensory walks', 'painter's palette', 'blindfold walk' and 'textural jigsaw' were used (Adams and Ward, 1982; Newcastle Architecture Workshop, 1982–1997). Reflecting on their experience, they made thoughtful interpretations of their environment through the media of art, dance and drama as well as discussion. One group developed memory maps, another produced a streamer dance in the playground. Through these experiences, they developed a shared vocabulary. A critical stance was encouraged. As awareness sharpened, pupils began to make judgements about environmental quality, starting from what they liked or disliked. They visited other environments and were able to make comparisons, developing critical skills. They observed how the grounds were used and carried out detailed measurements and site surveys, helped by a landscape architect (see Figure 14).

To help them generate ideas, children kept scrapbooks. Bubble plans were used to visualize size, scale and uses and how different activities might relate to each other. Children visited other school sites where improvements had been carried out to gather further ideas. They used tracing paper overlays on photographs to test out possibilities for change and to visualise what impact their ideas might have.

To develop and refine their ideas, children discussed the overall scheme, then chose particular elements within it, for which individual pupils produced detailed designs. Their ideas for seating, planting, entrances or sculpture were given to the landscape architect to incorporate in the overall design. Making models enabled the children to visualise change and facilitated lateral thinking and creative responses. Playground games were also used to examine relationships between people, spaces and activities.

An evaluation of the project was carried out in each school by means of an exhibition. In one school, representatives of the local authority, members of the local business community, governors, local councillors, education officers and parents attended the event. The plans were translated into community languages and interpreters were on hand to assist.

Figure 14 Children working with the Newcastle Architecture Workshop have opportunities to meet environmental professionals to discuss their work

Community development

The Community Development Project took place with a self-selected group of parents and friends of the school. Groups might comprise the local parish priest, the school caretaker, lunchtime supervisors, governors, playgroup leaders, teaching auxiliaries, parents and former parents. The aim was to involve the community in the design of improvements to the grounds and develop a group who would support the school in fundraising, maintenance and future development of the grounds.

Groups worked with the Newcastle Architecture Workshop for up to ten sessions and followed a similar programme to the pupils to engage them in the environmental design process. Greater emphasis was placed on the importance of play in child development and the relationship between environmental quality and play opportunity. Short-term improvements were planned and executed by the groups, including mural painting, and fundraising to purchase loose play equipment and maintain the gardens. Adults made a practical contribution, but also acted as valuable role models for the children. A landscape architect from the Newcastle Architecture Workshop participated in all the sessions with children, community and staff. This enabled all parties to understand her role in the process and work with her to develop an appropriate design brief.

Funding
The landscape plans were used as a vehicle for fundraising and to bid for funds from City Challenge to implement the schemes. The awards to individual schools varied, but a total of £240,000 has been invested to date by City Challenge. Schools found further funding through sources such as grant-making trusts, individual donations, sponsorship, fundraising events and contributions from their own budgets,

Implementation in schools: Hawthorn Primary School
Children and adult members of the school communities were involved wherever possible in implementing the changes. Improvements were usually complete within two years of the initial contact with the school. Hawthorn Primary School was one of the first to benefit from the scheme. Prior to the development, the school sports field had been unfenced and used as a dumping ground for burnt out cars and discarded rubbish. Pupils and teachers had suffered harassment from stray dogs and youths on motorbikes. The hard sports area was covered in broken glass and children had been confined to two small yards inside a stark perimeter fence. Planting had been neglected over the years and banks were bare and eroded.

The school was able to obtain a grant from a trust to pay for a landscape plan and some treeplanting. This was used to gain funding from City Challenge for further improvements. The grounds are now securely enclosed. The former sports field has an area of woodland, seats, paths and planting to create a community park. There is a hard sports court, early years play area, children's garden, picnic area and new planting beds. In fine weather, school meals are eaten at the picnic tables on the terrace outside the main entrance. The community park and sports area are open to the public until early evening as well as being used by the school for learning and teaching activities. The school has gone on to implement further improvements. A snack bar has been set up which is run and managed by the parents. Hawthorn Primary School now has a rising roll – a major achievement in a school threatened with closure prior to these changes.

Benefits

The Environmental Improvements Scheme has been positively received by the schools. It has created a safer, richer and more stimulating learning environment for the pupils. It has given pupils and other members of the school community a vivid experience of participation in environmental change, and made them aware of the satisfactions and frustrations which are a part of it. Schools report on the improved behaviour of children at playtimes and the wider variety of learning and social activities taking place. Some of those who had been involved in the school grounds courses are now involved in courses in adult education. Schools have also organised courses to equip parents with the skills to assist in the maintenance and management of the grounds.

TOWARDS EMPOWERMENT

Figure 15 Students in a design workshop at the Royal Academy of Arts discuss their ideas for a new bridge across the Thames

In Part III, experience of the case studies and similar work elsewhere has been distilled into a commentary and framework as a guide for others. Its aim is to offer practical advice as well as providing a theoretical underpinning for work with young people to enable them to participate in environmental planning.

Chapter 12 advises on the nature of the working relationships between young people, design and education professionals. Chapter 13 offers a framework for planning a project in schools which can also be adapted to other settings. The final chapter sums up with recommendations for policies and strategies to create a better support system for involving young people in environmental planning.

CHAPTER 12 Working together:
Professionals and young people

Young people's participation in environmental planning cannot happen without the encouragement, enthusiastic support and deliberate intervention of adults. This chapter explains how adults can facilitate young people's involvement in environmental planning. It focuses particularly on planners, teachers and young people in schools and considers the working relationships between them. However, much of the advice could apply to other professionals working with young people in other settings.

Environmental professionals

Officers from local authorities, in architecture and planning departments, leisure services, community development and environmental health, together with teachers in schools, researchers, youth and community workers and play workers, parents and elected members, all have a part to play in supporting young people's involvement in the planning process. Different kinds of professionals provide particular perspectives on the environment and bring to a working partnership with young people a wealth of experience and expertise. Planners, architects, landscape architects and artists have worked with teachers and young people in schools to develop environmental design projects. Youth workers have worked with a variety of community agencies to engage young people in developing a sense of place and thinking about possibilities for change.

Environmental professionals can help young people gain access to information, develop the knowledge to understand environmental issues and the skills to participate in the planning process. They can enable them to find their way through planning and political systems which often seem impenetrable to young people. Planners, housing officers, environmental health officers, surveyors and engineers have different areas of expertise. Planners and building surveyors are concerned to make the best use of land in urban and rural areas and to improve and conserve the environment. They have to consider the impact of development on the environment and take into account energy use and green issues. Architects design buildings and oversee their construction or conversion. They have technical knowledge of materials, construction, technology and law relating to buildings. Landscape architects are concerned with landscape quality, in the design of outdoor spaces, not only in parks, but in countryside conservation, roads and refurbishment of derelict industrial sites. Highway engineers consider the future traffic and transportation needs of an area, design new roads and other routes and maintain existing ones, keep records of traffic levels and accident statistics. Housing officers have a detailed knowledge of housing needs. Environmental health officers are concerned with monitoring and controlling pollution, including noise and emissions and with issues of public health. Elected members have knowledge of representation and how the decision-making process is conducted.

Teachers

Teachers have detailed knowledge of their pupils, their ability and what might be expected of them. They will know what previous work they have done, what knowledge and skills they can build on and what will be new to them. Teachers will be concerned that the work relates to the requirements of the National Curriculum and will concentrate on the knowledge, attitudes and skills which the pupils need to learn. They will also want to know what the results of a project might be and what levels of attainment their pupils might achieve. They will have a curriculum plan or programme of work to which the project will need to relate.

Teachers' professional expertise is evident in their working relationship with their pupils, particularly in their ability to devise methods for learning and strategies for teaching. They are able to create an appropriate environment for learning and define study tasks for their pupils. They are also experienced in organising groups of children to carry these out, and in overseeing the learning activities. They are able to explain to the children what is required, make appropriate demands on them and direct their efforts and energies.

Teachers' expertise is to be found not necessarily in their knowledge of the environment, but in an understanding of how children learn. Teachers tend to take their own professional skills for granted – how to address children and young people, how to stimulate and hold their interest and concentration, how to communicate with them, how to organise a group, how to support and direct a range of learning activities, how to juggle a range of interests and engagements at the same time, how to anticipate problems, how to deal with learning difficulties; these are all part of the teacher's daily routine. However clear the outsider might be in their presentations and explanations to children, a teacher will often have to interpret what has been said. This may be to clarify information or reinforce ideas. It may be because the teacher has sensed confusion or a lack of understanding, or knows that there are gaps in the pupils' knowledge.

Interprofessional collaboration

The efforts of environmental and design professionals are likely to be more successful if ways can be found to work across departmental and professional boundaries. Collaboration between different departments within a local authority, schools and youth organisations can achieve a great deal to provide opportunities and support for young people. This might result in the production of educational materials, the organisation of events and activities, the establishment of youth forums or environmental action groups or the development of live design and development projects.

Outsiders coming into schools are often referred to and treated as 'experts'. However, they may have little or no expertise in teaching or experience of working with young people outside their family circle. Planners and architects are not teachers or community workers. Everyone needs to be clear about what contribution different professionals can make to children's learning activity and to find ways of working together that are comfortable and complementary. Otherwise, outsiders may find themselves taking over the role of teacher, while the teacher plays policeman, storekeeper and troubleshooter. If the outsiders have all the fun and none of the responsibility teachers will end up feeling de-skilled and disenchanted (Adams, 1990a).

Roles

Adults can play a variety of roles in supporting young people's involvement in environmental planning, including those of facilitator, guide, interpreter and commentator. Sometimes they may deliberately play devil's advocate to challenge young people to think more fully about something. Or it might be that the adult takes on the role of manager, orchestrating a group of young people to work together. Adults may be involved as co-workers, contributing to the group effort in ways similar to the other participants, but with more experience and different kinds of expertise to contribute. They need to create opportunities for learning, to devise support systems and create ways through a complex field of study. Their role is multifaceted and includes that of mentor, information source, guide, supervisor, instructor, commentator, demonstrator, facilitator, referee, critic, interpreter and fellow traveller. Key roles are those of the enthusiast, expert, facilitator and educator.

Enthusiast

The nature of the working partnership between professionals and young people involved in environmental change cannot be described as a set of techniques or a list of 'do's' and 'dont's'. Underlying the relationship is the need for adults to value children's experience and perceptions and respect their views and opinions. Children and young people bring to the process of participation a lifetime's experience of their environment. They have their own perceptions, cultural perspectives and insights. Many of them have expert knowledge of their local neighbourhood, and are able to identify social and environmental issues which concern them. They possess enthusiasm and energy and are keen to do something to improve environmental quality: they look to the future with a sense of anticipation and excitement. But they can also be overwhelmed by the enormity of the environmental and social problems which exist. Faced with a diet of doom and gloom on the television or a concentration on problems in environmental education programmes, they may believe that they cannot do anything about the environmental issues which face society. They do not think that change is something over which they can have any control.

Adults need to engender a sense of optimism and hope, and encourage a positive view of the future. Above all, they need to present a positive attitude to change. Basic to the work of environmental designers such as planners, architects and landscape architects is the notion of generating and managing change. They need to communicate a sense of excitement and confidence in facing the future. They need to convey the idea that this is not something that happens to us, but something that we create. Adults need to appreciate the contribution young people can make. They must be committed to enabling them to play an active part in creating their own futures. Tokenism has no part to play here. It is not enough to go through the motions of consultation exercises with no conviction that they are worthwhile; this will not result in effective participation. Above all, adults need to inspire young people with a positive vision of the future and to create the motivation to encourage them in an area of community life which young people do not necessarily see as accessible.

Through their own enthusiasm, they can inspire young people, develop positive attitudes and motivate them to participate. They can provide role models, demonstrating ways of thinking and operating which will extend young people's ability to understand the environment and to take action in relation to it. This is more likely to happen through a direct working contact, but can also be achieved through organising events which welcome young people and by producing appropriate materials which convey the excitement and challenge of planning.

Expert

Environmental professionals may have professional experience and expertise in relation to the environment, but they are not necessarily experts on education or young people, especially those in the institutional setting of a group or the context of a youth group. They are not necessarily informed about how children or young people think or learn. However, environmental professionals can provide access to information and resources, making visible and comprehensible the planning system and the process of local government. So often, local government officers are content to hide in a large bureaucracy and avoid contact with the public, which they see as distracting them from their work. However, their work can be made more effective if people understand and appreciate what they are doing.

Although planning and environmental design can be incorporated as part of the programmes of study in the National Curriculum, neither primary nor secondary teachers are trained to teach them. Similarly, youth workers may have an interest, but their professional training does not enable them to offer adequate support to help young people participate in design or influence the decision-making process. Planners, architects and landscape architects, highway engineers, building surveyors, planning and development surveyors, housing officers and environmental health officers can:

- identify planning issues

- offer ways of thinking about environmental or behavioural change

- provide design expertise

- explain the decision-making process

Teachers and their pupils will expect planners and other design professionals to be expert on the planning system. Children and young people will want to know:

- What need is there for planning?

- What does a planner do?

- How does the planning process work?

- How are decisions made? Who decides? How?

- What happens when you submit a planning application?

- What is public consultation?

- What is the public enquiry process?

- How much do you earn?

Specialist vocabulary may need to be introduced. It may be necessary to make clear to both other adults and young people differences between development plans, structure plans, local plans, unitary development plans and development control. They may ask a whole range of questions such as: What is a development brief? What is a listed building or an industrial improvement area? How do you undertake environmental impact assessment? What is involved in an environmental enhancement scheme? Is a green wedge the same as green belt? What is the difference between officers and elected members? Who makes decisions about what the environment will look like? How much does it all cost? Environmental professionals will need to be prepared to answer such questions, and to explain complex ideas and systems in a straightforward way.

Facilitator

As facilitators and managers, adults can create opportunities, strategies and mechanisms for young people's participation. It is particularly useful when planners can offer live local projects as a focus for participation, and is more likely to result in the learning experience being vivid and meaningful. Professionals from different agencies and disciplines can provide access to information, resources, materials and people. They can identify different sources of information about the environment, design, local policies, planning and local government. Young people need to know how to gain access to information and knowledge, whether it be located in libraries, planning departments or the Internet. They need to be alerted to professional contacts and networks, local and regional and national agencies, environmental community and voluntary groups, young people's organisations, professional associations and other non-governmental organisations. Planners can provide liaison between departments, agencies and professions to create a support network for young people's involvement in environmental planning.

Educator

In an educational role, planners and other professionals can help young people think about environmental issues, the conflicts of interest and the solutions that are possible. They can demonstrate techniques and methods not only to help young people research issues and investigate problems but engage them in the design process, concerned with dealing with change. And they can help them find a way through the system to make sure their views are communicated to other members of the community, officers and elected members.

Communication is a key consideration in developing a good working relationship. It is easy to talk *at* children and young people. It is easy to *tell* them things. It is easy to talk *about* things that interest you, that may have no meaning for them. There is a need to engage young people in a dialogue and oblige them to think, through questioning, discussion and argument. It is helpful if professionals engage in debate with young people about environmental issues and help them formulate their own opinions and develop reasoned arguments to justify them. To do this, adults need to encourage young people to formulate the questions to ask rather than have all the answers themselves. Often it is necessary to build on what they know, to reinforce existing knowledge and skills. At other times it is important to challenge them, to expose them to unfamiliar ideas and ways of thinking so that they can develop the skills necessary for participation.

Role model

Environmental designers such as architects, planners and landscape architects have a positive attitude to change. They see problems as spurs to action. Their work centres on problem-solving techniques and how to resolve conflicts of interest. It is important for young people to see adults as optimistic, realistic, practical and helpful. The working contact may be through projects in school, or where young people have opportunities for work experience in a planning department, an architect's office or a local authority office.

In helping young people to develop the skills and capabilities necessary for participation, adults need to demonstrate the model of the good learner. They need to show young people how to confront new experience and engage with unfamiliar ideas, how to assimilate them, and how to invest new understanding in further action. This means that the traditional form of teaching and learning – the transmission, absorption and regurgitation of information – has to be replaced with a generative mode of working. This involves generating and sharing experience, reflecting upon it, appraising it and reworking it to create shared knowledge and meaning. It means providing young people with feedback and helping them take a critical stance to their own work.

Working with young people

It may be very difficult for outsiders to go into schools or youth clubs and work with young people. They may know very little about young people in groups in institutional or community settings. So often, adults coming into schools have unrealistic expectations. They are surprised when young people appear not to know very much about their particular area of expertise. They use language that young people do not seem to understand. They find it odd that young people do not know how the planning system or the decision-making process works. They are surprised that young people's ideas sometimes seem so conventional, and that they cannot see alternative possibilities. They are surprised by the limitations and constraints set by the timetable and the programme of the school day. Or they are disappointed when young people in a youth group appear at a meeting to be enthusiastic, then do not show up for a while. They can be taken aback by young people's passivity and their reluctance to question or they can be shocked by their honesty, their forthright and uncompromising manner. There is no formula for success. All young people are different and each group will require a different approach.

It is important to establish a working relationship quickly. Use any appropriate technique to learn everyone's names – badges, labels, annotated plans of the work area – addressing people by their names at every opportunity. The adults will be learning as much about the young people as they will be learning about planning. It is helpful if participants relate to each other as co-workers in a shared enterprise; professionals should not be afraid to ask young people for help or support. Adults should be ready to make demands, engage the young people actively and directly and enable them to take responsibility for their own learning.

Planning issues

Built environment professionals can help young people identify and explore issues which relate to relationships between people and their surroundings: the way we shape and control the environment, the way resources are allocated and used, and the need for change. Planning issues might focus on proposals for new development, improvement or conservation schemes. Figure 16 provides a list of possible areas for study.

access and disability	*land availability and*	*public transport*
children's environments	*allocation*	*recycling*
conservation	*leisure and recreational*	*road safety*
cultural amenities	*facilities*	*safety and security*
educational facilities	*nature conservation*	*school grounds*
employment	*open space*	*shopping*
energy	*pedestrianisation*	*sustainability*
housing	*play provision*	*tourism*
infill development	*pollution*	*traffic and transport*

Figure 16 Possible areas for study with young people

Resources

Local authorities and environmental groups hold vast amounts of information on the environment, so it is not always necessary to undertake original research. Planning departments have information useful to young people engaged in environmental projects, including maps, plans, photographs, newspaper articles, census data, population projections, historical records, surveys, reports, studies, leaflets, information on planning legislation and environmental standards and monitoring, as well as guidance on design. Other departments such as environmental health will probably have information on litter, recycling, waste management, green issues, public health, food hygiene and packaging.

It is important for young people to learn to use secondary sources of information, which can be found in publications and computer data banks. Here, it will be necessary for them to learn how to access information, as well as how to interpret the ways in which it is recorded. So often a lot of energy goes into collecting information, but the way it is analysed and interpreted requires careful consideration. In researching environmental topics, it is particularly important to be able to distinguish between information and propaganda.

However, the information to be found in local authorities may not be in a form suitable for use by school pupils. There may be copyright restrictions; the cost of retrieving the information for schools may be prohibitive; there may be confidentiality restrictions on the information; or it may not correspond with the geographical areas in which the young people are interested. Planning departments have to consider how much time and resources they can allocate to securing information for the public. Some make a charge to cover the cost of photocopying, while others add the cost of time and effort.

A good use of resources and a way of cutting down officers' time on tracking down and sorting out information is to create a collection of resources for use by young people, which would be derived from materials to be found in various departments in local authorities. These may be developed into a series of packs, for instance, on planning, environmental health, transport, green issues and housing. This should be done through an interprofessional group of built environmental professionals, teachers, youth workers and community development workers. When compiling material, be clear what it is for. Does it provide data and information? Does it explain methods for investigation? Does it help young people explore issues? Avoid doing all the work for the children. It is all too easy to put together packs and kits that provide information, offer explanation and do all the thinking. In themselves these are not necessarily educational; children do not learn by absorption. You will need to question whether the materials will engage them in active learning, help them find out things, weigh up evidence, make judgements, and develop the capacity for critical thought. The age, gender and ability of the children will need to be considered and whether the materials have already been tested out by children.

Schools will have a library and some reference material. They are not likely to have a collection of resources for local study or environmental issues. Local authority officers can help them establish a useful resource collection of materials for studying the local area and exploring environmental issues. Local authority teachers' centres and urban studies centres sadly are ceasing to exist. However, this does not mean that there is no need for them. Through the efforts of a keen enthusiast, a particular school may establish itself as a central focus for a cluster of schools or a geographical area as an environmental resource centre. Master copies of materials supplied by local authority officers could be lodged there and used by teachers and others to create suitable learning materials for children.

Networks

Environmental professionals involved in education and public participation tend to develop a network of local contacts. These include teachers in schools, local education authority advisers and inspectors, headteachers' forums and governors' associations. It may be helpful to contact national organisations such as teachers' professional associations, e.g. National Association for Environmental Education (NAEE), environmental designers' own professional organisations such as branches of the Royal Town Planning Institute (RTPI) and the Royal Institute of British Architects (RIBA), regional environmental education agencies such as Groundwork, and national environmental organisations such as the Council for Environmental Education (CEE) and the National Association for Urban Studies (NAUS). These people and agencies can provide valuable information and advice.

Making contact

Is there a policy in place which supports local authority officers' educational work with local communities? An approach might come from a school to a local authority department. This may be delightfully vague, such as, 'Do you have anything on housing?' (or pollution or transport). Resist the urge to say something rude and ask for a few more details. What kind of project are the children doing? Are some general ideas or suggestions on current issues what is wanted or is specific information on particular developments required? What kinds of resources are needed? Maps or plans? Photographs or reports?

Historical or current surveys? Would a list of resources be helpful? Would some of the council's free leaflets be useful? Explain the costs involved and make a note of the caller's name, school and telephone number.

You also need to think about your own mechanisms for dealing with such requests. Is there a system in place to deal with requests for information from schools? Is there anyone whose responsibility it is to deal with these? How are requests for contact with planners dealt with? Is the response done as a favour or is there a system in place where time and resources are allocated for public information or education initiatives? Most of the time, people do not know what to ask for because they do not know what enquiries are appropriate or what material might be made accessible. Is there a collection of free leaflets and brochures produced by the local authority or a simple directory of resources which could be made available? Are there lists of local contacts and national organisations which might be able to help?

Approaching schools and youth organisations

If planners, architects or landscape architects wish to establish contact with young people, this can be done through local schools, youth groups or youth organisations. A direct approach to the adults responsible is appropriate. In schools, the first contact will be with the headteacher. However, it is important to make personal contact with the individual teachers concerned as soon as possible. Some schools have designated members of staff, e.g. coordinators with special responsibility for environmental education, but there may also be others who wish to be involved. If you telephone a school, do not be surprised if you find difficulty in reaching the teacher you want to speak to. Very few schools have telephones in the classroom. If you send a fax or letter, make sure it identifies clearly who the respondent is, otherwise communications will be lost in the day-to-day business of the school. Posters and leaflets sent for display on the noticeboard may also get lost unless they are the responsibility of a particular teacher. Making contact is the first step. The next is to establish common concerns and create a framework for planning a project.

CHAPTER 13 Project planning, organisation and development

The aim in this chapter is to provide a framework to help organisers consider the thinking and the practicalities involved in planning and organising a project and to anticipate some possible outcomes. It alerts them to the possibilities and constraints involved in organising work with pupils and what might be necessary in project development. Not all projects will include all of the processes or phases described in the framework. The balance and bias of the work will be different depending on the subject under investigation, the people involved and the problems they have set themselves. The framework concentrates on collaboration between architects, planners, teachers and pupils in schools and is focused primarily on participation in environmental design. However, it could apply to other settings.

Planning a project

The subsections below describe some of the practicalities and issues to be considered when planning a project. These are also represented in Figure 17 (pp. 138–139).

First meetings

Although it is helpful for the environmental professional to see the school and understand the context in which children will be working, the first meetings with a teacher are more likely to be productive if they are not during lesson time, when the teacher will have other concerns and responsibilities. It may be more appropriate to have a relaxed yet focused brainstorming session with the teacher, generating ideas for study and considering alternatives before deciding on a particular route. The teacher will need to do more detailed planning, fitting the timing and programming of the work into the demands of the timetable and the busy school day and relating the content of the study to the requirements of the National Curriculum. Further meetings will be necessary to clarify the aims and objectives and the various stages involved.

Environmental professionals and teachers need to decide on the scope of the work, the focus and direction the study will take and, importantly, what the pupils will learn from the experience. Teachers will be particularly interested in the kinds of attitudes, skills and understandings that children will develop to enable them to participate more effectively in the future. Environmental professionals may be more interested in their opinions and proposals which can be fed into the planning process immediately. These are not incompatible, but it is important to remember that planners, teachers and young people might have very different reasons and motivations for engaging in an environmental project.

A few reminders about schools

There are great differences in how learning is organised in primary and secondary schools. In primary schools, class teachers are responsible for teaching all the subjects in the National Curriculum, though they may have a particular specialisation. They will be particularly concerned to develop language and numeracy skills, and will be keen that these should come into play in any project. In secondary schools, teachers will be responsible for a particular subject area. In both primary and secondary schools, there may be a coordinator responsible for environmental education. There may be other teachers responsible for personal and social education and citizenship. In secondary schools, the environmental education coordinator will probably have a science or geography background, though there may be teachers from other subjects with a personal and professional interest in the environment. Planners and other environmental professionals may find themselves acting as a catalyst to enable teachers from different disciplines to work together.

National Curriculum

Environmental education is firmly in the National Curriculum. However, teachers will need to satisfy themselves how an environmental planning project can fit into the curriculum and relate to the requirements imposed by programmes of study and Ofsted inspections. It will be necessary to decide which subject areas will be involved. A historical perspective might be useful. Design will involve thinking about change. Art will be needed to perceive the environment as it is and also to visualise the impact of possible changes. Maths will be involved in dealing with measurements, scales, costs or statistics. Geography will be useful if mapping and surveys are involved. Pupils will need various kinds of language skills to carry out investigations and to communicate their ideas.

Programming

Project organisers need to decide how long the project will take and how time will be allocated. It will probably have to be fitted into primary school project work or the traditional secondary school timetable of one or two lessons each week. However, it is likely to require 'block' timetabling to create half-day study sessions to permit greater continuity and depth of study. Timing is important. During the school year, the three terms, autumn, spring and summer, have a different character. If work on site is planned, this is probably best done at the beginning of the autumn or summer terms, so that the development work can take place later in the term. It is not a good idea to start an environmental project requiring fieldwork in January, because of the poor weather. Older pupils in secondary schools are involved in examinations for most of the summer term. However, July might be a time to run field courses or develop induction courses focused on environmental study, for older pupils who wish to continue their studies in further education.

Study area
In recent years, schools have found it more and more difficult to organise off-site visits because of transport difficulties, costs, health and safety regulations, difficulties with supervision and constraints of time. However, many schools acknowledge the value of using the environment as an educational resource and are willing to make every effort to accommodate work off-campus. In selecting a study area, it is important to consider how easily this can be accessed by the pupils. How familiar or unfamiliar it is to them may have implications for the kinds of study methods employed. It is important to consider how many visits will be necessary and anticipate the implications in terms of time, costs or organisation. Permissions may need to be sought from parents and owners or managers of a particular site. There are health and safety regulations which need to be addressed.

Pupils
Teachers should be consulted on the kinds of projects possible with particular age groups and what depth of study is appropriate. Outsiders' expectations of children's abilities can be inaccurate. Environmental professionals sometimes expect children to know more than they do or be capable of doing things they have not yet attempted. Or expectations may be too low, so that children are not stretched or challenged to develop their ability to think. In planning a study, the age and ability of the pupils need to be taken into account, as does their experience of previous environmental projects. There should be opportunities for them to contribute to the process of planning the project, particularly when they may have expert knowledge of the local area.

Aims and objectives

Broad aims can be translated into specific objectives and short-term goals. Pupils need to understand what they might learn from the project. Planning the project should take account of the content of the study, clearly identifying the ideas with which the young people will engage. Adults supporting the work should anticipate what learning activities and teaching strategies may be used. Young people will learn about the design process, the decision-making process and the planning system not through description or explanation, but primarily through participation. This is one area of the curriculum where it is important for young people of all ages to learn by doing. In planning a programme of work or sequence of learning activities, five distinct, yet linked, areas of study should be considered: *awareness and response*; *perception*; *critique*; *design activity*; and *communication*. Each could form the basis for a discrete project, developing particular understandings and skills which come into play at various stages in the process of participation. As a sequence, they are likely to result in an experience of participation which has some degree of depth and meaning for the young person.

Skills and capacities

Each of these areas involves a range of skills and capabilities which are acquired through experience and developed through practice. It is not only the development of intellectual skills that will be important. Problem identification and problem solving require pupils to make connections, develop insights, make informed guesses and follow up hunches, which might also involve empathy and intuition. Social and interpersonal skills are required in team working and group decision-making.

Perceptual, analytical and interpretive skills

Young people's powers of observation and analysis should be sharpened to increase their awareness of the world around them. A personal, feeling response should be encouraged to develop a sense of place. The aim should be to extend their understanding of environmental issues and encourage a concern for environmental quality. Certain types of investigative skills may be developed, for instance, through the use of questionnaires, interviews, map reading, traffic counts and land use surveys. Perceptual, analytical and interpretive skills can be developed through direct engagement with primary sources by means of annotated sketches and documentary photography, or through the use of secondary source material, using historical and statistical data.

Figure 17 (above and opposite) Planning a project (from Adams and Kean, 1991)

ROLES AND RESPONSIBILITIES

LEARNING + TEACHING METHODS

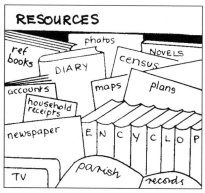

RESOURCES

EQUIPMENT, MATERIALS

DOCUMENTATION, EVALUATION

SHARING EXPERIENCE

Critical skills

Young people will need to develop discriminatory skills and systems of appraisal or critique to make informed judgements and develop the capacity for reasoned argument. This is more likely to happen in the context of group work, where ideas and opinions are shared and compared. Young people should be encouraged to support their views with evidence, to explain and justify how they have arrived at them.

Design capability

Design is primarily concerned with dealing with change. Involvement in design activity develops young people's abilities to hypothesise, to visualise alternative or future possibilities and to test out ideas, imagining the potential for change. Imagination and fantasy play a part here, as do technical skills, all of which are developed through drawings, plans, photography and constructions. The use of computers is a growing influence in this area of study, providing opportunities to generate, develop and test out ideas before putting them into practice.

Communication skills

Young people need to be able to present and communicate their views effectively. This needs to be done through the spoken or written word in seminars and reports, but also through visual and spatial means, using maps, plans, diagrams, graphs and models.

Roles and responsibilities

Organisers will need to decide who will do what, and at what points in the project other environmental professionals should be involved. Key opportunities are at the briefing, the site investigation, interrogation of evidence, defining the design problem, determining possible solutions, presentation and critique of the work and in preparing material to communicate to people outside the school. Similarities and differences between the roles of the different professionals involved need to be clarified and potential conflicts avoided.

Resources

Material will be needed for background information, data, reference, comparison or as exemplars. Resources might be used by the teacher or environmental professional as part of an explanation or demonstration – film and video can provide useful stimulus. Resources will be needed by pupils for self-directed study. They may need to refer to an exhibition or display for ready reference or informal learning opportunities or have access to maps, plans, photographs and historical reference material. Current reference books and other documents such as reports, or explanatory leaflets, may be identified by the environmental professional, as specialist or technical information on materials, planning regulations and ergonomics will not be readily available in schools.

With some support, teachers can be encouraged to develop resource banks of material, including pupils' work, and to create databases in card indexes or on computer files, or make reference collections of photographs, maps and other documentation. Young people should be able to contribute to this process. The experience of organising, collecting and retrieving information will be invaluable for them in future study activities. These resources can be used by other teachers. Any handouts which are prepared should be carefully conserved so that they can be copied or adapted for future projects. Information and documentation made available by environmental professionals may be of interest not only to children and young people, but to their parents and other adults visiting the school. The school could become another point of information for the community and engage people in planning matters. The investment of time in putting together materials for a particular project can have a long-term impact on the work of others.

Materials and equipment

It may be appropriate for pupils to build up project files which they can retain. In secondary schools, these may form part of their coursework for examination or inspection purposes. Loose leaf ring-binders are useful here, but it may also be necessary to keep work in group portfolios. Added to these, the cost of pens, paper, card, acetates, photographic materials, folders, storage boxes, adhesive, glue guns and cutting tools and perhaps more substantial modelling materials such as balsa wood can mount up alarmingly. However, effective use of design techniques and the use of good quality graphic materials can do a lot to create good results. Equipment may include audiovisual equipment such as cameras and projectors, computers and photocopiers. It may be necessary to arrange for pupils to be able to make use of these.

Costs

The costs of the project need to be calculated. Appropriate headings need to be identified within the school budget. The cost of the time spent in schools by outside professionals may have to be paid for. The cost of supply cover to release teachers for meetings or to accompany groups out of school may be covered by the budget for in-service training and professional development. Schools may take advantage of concessions for group travel to offset transport costs. Money needs to be found to document work in progress. The material generated can then be used in exhibitions and documents to share what has been learned with other teachers and pupils in the school, as well as to inform parents, governors and other members of the community. It can also be used as a resource for work by other groups of children.

Documentation

Documenting young people's efforts will provide useful feedback and enable them to reflect on their experience so that they can learn from it. Documentation will provide evidence of study and an explanation of the process of learning as well as an indication of outcomes. It will embody young people's ideas and opinions as well as those of the adults involved. Pupils should be encouraged to document their own work to enable them to become aware of the need to take responsibility for their own learning. Such activity also helps the adults involved to become reflective practitioners, self-critical and able to learn from experience.

Evaluation

Instead of thinking about evaluation after completing a project, it is important to build in systems at the beginning, so that monitoring and evaluation are seen as an integral part of the development of the work. It is necessary to monitor progress if only to decide what to do next, contributing to the process of formative evaluation, to inform the development of the work. The focus for evaluation may be on the ideas that are being explored. What consideration is being given to people's needs? Will the proposals result in improvements in environmental quality? Are the ideas original, interesting, challenging or pedestrian and derivative, feasible or practicable? Have both benefits and problems been considered? Are the methods of presentation original, informative or illuminating? What depth of study is evident? Alternatively, the focus may be on ways of working and the interactions within the group. Have the investigative methods been appropriate? Have the young people worked effectively as members of a group? What have been the strength or weakness of individual contributions? What skills, capabilities or understanding can transfer to other situations?

In summative evaluation, the quality of the work is assessed. This will involve consideration of both the content of the ideas and how they are communicated. What will pupils understand or know that they did not know before? What concepts or ideas will they be able to think about? What will they be able to do that they could not do before? What will be their attitudes to the environment, to change or to planning for the future when they have completed the project? Will they have learnt new ideas, concepts or skills? When their work on the project is assessed, who will make the judgements? Will it be through peer review or adults' comments? What will be the criteria for assessment? It is important that the young people themselves should be encouraged to reflect on their experience to reinforce their understanding and their sense of achievement. Adults too should think about what they have learnt and whether it will affect their work in the future

Sharing experience

There is a great joy in achievement, but it is made all the sweeter if others can share it. It is important for young people to disseminate the results of their efforts. Parents, governors and others in the education field will be interested in the work and how the young people have been able to develop the skills necessary for effective participation. If a key concern is to create opportunities for children and young people to participate in environmental planning and make their views known to the decision-makers, then the mechanisms for feedback to planning departments, planning committees and elected members should be clear at the outset. Sometimes, this will be through correspondence or informal reports. It may be mediated by the adults working with the young people, or communicated directly by the young people themselves through presentations in meetings. The encouragement and interest of adults motivates children and helps validate their work.

Young people may just wish to extend the debate. Now that schools are increasingly using computers, and many have access to e-mail and the Internet, it is possible to make contact with people further afield. Environmental issues offer an inexhaustible fund of issues to discuss with others, both in the UK and abroad. It might be important to make contact with other young people locally. Using the local press is one possibility, with a young people's page written by themselves. Leaflets, brochures and newsletters can all be used to disseminate a group's ideas and report on its activities. It is useful if these are illustrated, as it identifies those who are involved and gives a picture of their activities. Notice boards in school, youth club or library may be a good way of making local contacts or extending membership of the group. Groups have found the support of the local media very helpful. The preparation of a press release to coincide with a key event or important initiative may create interest and will provide useful copy. Local newspapers, radio and television welcome positive news stories from young people and may produce material which groups will be able to use in further dissemination. This may add support for their work in future.

At the beginning of a project all this may seem a long way off; however, it is useful to anticipate what might be possible outcomes of all the effort involved.

Organising work with pupils

Involving young people in the planning and organisation of the work is important as a first step in participation. The emphasis should be on active learning, where young people are encouraged to understand ideas through investigation and develop their thinking through comparison and critique, working together to test out ideas and generate meanings. These experiences contribute to the development of different forms of 'literacy': verbal, visual and environmental. What is described is a reiterative process, where there is constant questioning, critique and testing of ideas to inform the development of the work. Adults can help young people focus on environmental issues, engage them in debate and enable them to formulate their own opinions and develop strong arguments to justify them. It is useful for young people to have adults to advise on developing a framework for action, as they are likely to anticipate the problems and difficulties young people may face. To do this, adults will need to help young people frame appropriate questions instead of having all the answers.

The subsections below describe the main aspects of working with pupils, and then the section on Project Development looks at the content and themes which are common to most environmental projects. Figure 18 (pp. 146–147) high-lights the main ideas described in both sections.

Introduction and briefing

The introduction to the project will need to stimulate young people's interest and engender enough enthusiasm for them to want to participate. The project may build on local interests and current events, to which they can easily relate, or it may introduce them to more distant and complex issues. Think about how the ideas will be introduced – through a lecture, or a film, a slide presentation, an exhibition or a debate. The intentions of the project need to be clearly explained, and may be set out in the form of a study brief, which clarifies the questions to be addressed or issues to be investigated. The participants may need help in understanding the brief and how it relates to the short- and long-term goals of the project.

Streetwork

The research methods need to be clearly understood. Before conducting investigations, young people may need to have briefing notes or work sheets in addition to verbal instructions and advice. Some may already have the knowledge and skills to do the work, while others may need to learn new techniques – will they learn these first then apply them afterwards, or learn them 'on the job' through undertaking surveys or appraisals? Think about how the streetwork sessions and site visits will be organised and who will be responsible for them. Remember that teachers may be extremely difficult to contact at school, and it may not be easy for them to make arrangements with individuals or agencies outside school.

Classwork

Classwork will need to be organised to develop the ideas and address the issues raised through the initial investigations. Will there be opportunities for class teaching, individual study and group work? In what ways will pupils be involved in generating ideas? What techniques will they use to analyse and appraise material? How far will they need to rely on primary data sources? How much will they use secondary sources of information? It may be necessary to check that the school or local library is able to deal with their enquiries and that the young people are able to access the information available. Will they need to know how to undertake computer searches or use CD-ROMs? Will they need to interview people? Also, think about how discussion sessions will be handled. Some teachers are not used to having other adults working alongside them, so it may be necessary to experiment with different roles and activities to arrive at a comfortable accommodation.

Group work

Participation is not a solitary exercise. It is done within a social context and requires collaborative working within a group. Participating in a group develops a range of interpersonal and language skills which can transfer to other situations. Pupils should understand the reasons for working in a group and should be clear what the study tasks are. They may have to negotiate how the group operates, the contribution and responsibilities of each participant and the role of the adults who are supporting the work. Time will be needed for exploring ideas, for discussion and debate. Argument should be used to shape and develop thinking. If the focus is environmental issues, words might be sufficient to share ideas, but design activity will require pupils to use drawing and modelling techniques. Groups will need to decide on how to deal with

Figure 18 (above and opposite) Organising work with pupils, and project development

DESIGN ACTIVITY TO GENERATE, TEST, DEVELOP PROPOSALS for CHANGE

DISCUSSION, ARGUMENT

COMMUNICATION, CRITIQUE

SHARING IDEAS WITH THE COMMUNITY, ACTION, IMPLEMENTATION

NEIGHBOUR- HOOD CHANGE

disagreements and differences of opinion and how to decide on a plan of action. It can be helpful to have a series of short-term goals which are achievable, to create steps upon the way to achieving the larger aims. Grand plans that fail can lead to disappointment, frustration and projects being abandoned. It is also important to prioritise concerns and initiatives. Sometimes adults can support the decision-making process by doing nothing; so often the temptation is to intervene to help things along. However, it is useful if young people can learn by understanding group dynamics, working through difficulties and finding ways of resolving conflicts themselves.

Independent learning

Young people will also need encouragement and support to become independent learners, able to construct investigations and take control of their own learning activity. So often in schools, study is closely directed. Environmental projects offer opportunities for independent enquiry, when pupils are motivated to seek out information and generate material not readily available in school. Often, they enlist the help of family and neighbours. Interviewing, contacting organisations, identifying resources, collecting newspaper cuttings, taking photographs, watching television programmes on related themes, are all activities which the participants may do outside lesson time to contribute to a project.

Project development

The following framework for project development is based on the idea of young people working with teachers and environmental professionals on an environmental design project which will probably involve:

- developing environmental awareness
- critique, raising issues
- identifying need or opportunity for change
- design activity
- decision-making
- communication and outcomes

Environmental awareness

The projects described in Part II indicate a wide range of environments where young people have contributed to thinking about change in residential neighbourhoods, school environments, town centres and shopping areas, parks and countryside, all of them places which are part of their lives. Young people care what they look like, what they feel like and what happens to them. What draws people to places and makes them connect with them? What creates strong emotional engagement with the environment? How do we feel a sense of being located in and belonging to a particular environment? Why do we care about places? What meanings and significance do particular places have for us? Sense of place may be a difficult concept to explain, yet it influences much of young people's motivation in wanting to be involved in shaping and controlling their local environment.

Sense of place
Young people's experience of the environment is very different from that of adults. Environmental change should take account of the experience and knowledge they have of their locality. Surveys and audits, questionnaires and interviews are all excellent techniques to record information, but sometimes they are not appropriate to explore the subtle and hidden feelings that connect us with a place. They do not reveal the experiences and memories of childhood and youth that contribute to creating a sense of place.

Strategies
Here, art, drama, storytelling and poetry can illuminate the relationships between people and place more powerfully. Sensory walks, memory maps, photographic essays and video diaries have enabled young people to record their experience of particular environments. Through writing poetry or telling stories, they are able to reflect on their experience and make sense of it. They are also interested in adults' accounts of their own childhoods. Oral history projects where younger people document the reminiscences of older people are popular. Hearing about other people's stories creates an empathy with people and place. Learning about the history of an area locates it in a wider context and gives their own efforts a new significance, as part of the evolution of change. It is important to value what is positive in a place before embarking on a process of change, to know what people are thinking or how they act before attempting to change their attitudes or behaviours.

Communicate
Drawings, video diaries, illustrated neighbourhood maps, photo exhibitions for display in the school or the local library can all be created by young people. Brochures and booklets can be written and illustrated by children and perhaps published with the help of local sponsorship. These may act as a trigger to

encourage others in the community to look again at a familiar environment and perhaps perceive it afresh and value it more.

Raising issues

Most children and young people are reliant on television to inform their view of the world. How are built environment and social concerns portrayed on the television? How does television present environmental issues? Much of the emphasis is on endangered wildlife, disappearing habitats, pollution and so on. It is more likely that television and newspapers will report on major environmental disasters rather than local achievements. The urban environment is also likely to be seen as negative. Advertising is another branch of the media which communicates powerful ideas about the environment and the way we should live. It presents young people with a bewildering range of lifestyles and tempting escapist consumer fantasies. How do these shape their view of the environment and what the future should be like?

Environmental education

At school, young people are exposed to local concerns and global environmental issues through environmental education programmes. Research from the Henley Centre for Forecasting (1991) indicates that school projects and lessons are young people's main source of information relating to environmental issues. It also indicates that 60 per cent of the children surveyed do not consider that enough is taught in relation to the environment. Environmental organisations produce educational materials and some have sections which young people can join. However, conservation issues can emphasise problems so much that young people feel unable to do anything about the world's problems. Dealing with change is an important part of environmental education, yet this is so often presented in the context of technological solutions to environmental problems, ignoring what are, in essence, human and cultural ones.

Strategies

A 'news watch' is useful to explore environmental issues. Groups might choose to focus on the television, local press or national press or choose particular magazines and over a period of a month, create a collection of articles and images about anything to do with the environment. An 'issues wall' can be created by building up a collection of cuttings, perhaps with illustrations and comments attached. The next stage is to undertake some form of analysis. Are the articles mostly positive or negative? What countries do they feature? What are the key problems which are identified? What are governments and organisations trying to do about the problems? What are individuals trying to do? Or maybe the focus could be the local area and the material derived primarily from local newspapers. This could be a good starting point for discussion. The role of the adults here is to stimulate discussion, ask questions, present counter-arguments and help young people develop reasoned judgement. Alternatively, simulations and role play enable young people to play out the roles of the various groups involved in an environmental issue, articulating the arguments, exploring alternatives, and perhaps finding a way through to conflict resolution.

Research

Access to information and resources

Young people need to know how to gain access to information and knowledge, whether it be located in libraries, planning departments, or the Internet. Adults can also provide access to professional contacts and networks, including individuals, planning, local and national government agencies, environmental, community and voluntary groups, children's organisations, professiónal associations and other nongovernmental organisations.

Collecting information and opinion

It is important that children and young people are involved in formulating the questions to be asked and that they understand the need for the research. It is also important that they understand the methods used in the research, so that they can use them appropriately. Both quantitative and qualitative data will probably be important and require different methods to generate the research material. Quantitative studies might include monitoring environmental quality and the use of resources through surveys and audits, researching air pollution, air and water quality, litter, energy conservation, vandalism and graffiti. Qualitative studies may include interviews to gather opinion from different interest groups such as residents, children or shop-keepers. Young people can undertake different kinds of environmental audits and surveys. They might also use questionnaires to gather information or conduct interviews to find out people's opinions. This technique should be properly supervised by adults so that young people are not put at risk in approaching strangers. Photographic diaries, journals and studies based on young people's own experience of places are particularly valuable, as this kind of material revealing young people's perceptions of place is difficult to find.

Environmental impact is an important aspect of planners' work. They can suggest various techniques and methods to monitor, measure and evaluate environmental quality. They can help identify the research questions to be addressed. What are you trying to find out? What kinds of information are required? What methods and techniques are appropriate for exploration and investigation? Techniques may include land use surveys, traffic counts, parking surveys, shopping surveys, transport user survey, interviews and polls. The process of gathering data about the environment or organising investigations to explore and understand how people perceive their environment, how they use or abuse it, raises awareness of issues. It is important that young people understand that proposals for change should be based on sound knowledge of the existing situation, or there is a danger of inflicting more damage leading to greater environmental degradation. A careful analysis and interpretation of findings from investigations can identify a need or opportunity for change.

Analysing, interpreting and evaluating information
The collection and analysis of the information is the first stage. The material, whether it be photographs, the results of questionnaires, transcripts of interviews or maps of land use, needs to be interpreted and evaluated for young people to make sense of it and determine how it can feed into the thinking about the need or opportunity for change.

Identify need or opportunity for change

Critique
The need or opportunity for change should be determined after consultation with others and through a careful analysis of their views. It will probably be necessary to consider the results of research, opinion gathering and local policies before deciding on the need for change. Adults can help young people develop appropriate criteria for judgement.

The need for environmental change may emerge because there is a problem, or a local issue which needs attention. For example, there is no safe place for young children to play in the neighbourhood, the school playground is featureless and boring, with nowhere to sit and chat to friends, or there is a problem with traffic in residential streets. Alternatively, local development or regeneration initiatives may throw up possibilities for environmental improvements. For instance, a supermarket has plans to build a new store in the high street or a new housing development is scheduled for vacant land. How might the development create a child-friendly environment? Where might young people be able to make a positive contribution to the thinking about design? An excellent

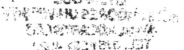

starting point is the school site. Through various kinds of appraisal techniques, investigations into design and layout and climate conditions, as well as analysis of the use of the site and the impact of aesthetic and design quality, it is possible to recognise the strengths and weaknesses of the site and begin to identify the need or opportunity for change.

Consultation

Any discussion on environmental issues, or sharing of viewpoints about places, will reveal that people have very different perceptions, informed by different values. They have different needs and requirements, aspirations and fears. There is a need to establish common ground, identify conflicts and find areas of compromise. The question to ask is not 'what do we want?' but 'what does the community need?'. Careful thought must be given to the form and nature of the consultation which young people can organise for themselves. Who will it involve? Will it involve adults as well as other young people? Will it give due regard to the view of males and females, young and old, or is it targeted at particular groups? Will it be carried out through questionnaires, structured interviews with individuals or meetings with groups?

Design activity

Generate ideas

Scrapbooks, research notebooks and collections of images are useful as a source of inspiration to generate ideas and help young people think about change. In environmental design, bubble plans can be used to visualise how different activities might relate to each other. Brainstorming and group discussions are necessary, where ideas and notes are recorded to show the range and development of ideas, so that they can be shared and manipulated by the group. Visits to other places may be appropriate to gather more ideas. The emphasis is on generating a number of options.

Develop ideas

To develop and refine ideas, it will be necessary for the group to analyse features, compare qualities and discuss the overall scheme, particular elements of which can then be selected for more detailed work. Tracing paper overlays can be used on photographs to test out possibilities for change and to visualise what impact proposals for change might have. Making models creates opportunities to visualise change in 3-D and can facilitate lateral thinking and encourage creative responses.

LIVERPOOL
JOHN MOORES UNIVERSITY
AVRIL ROBARTS LRC
TEL. 0151 231 4022

Critique

There is a need to evaluate ideas at many stages of the design process. Change does not necessarily imply improvement. It is important to consider the possible impact of proposals before putting them into action. In environmental design, it is not possible to create a prototype and test it out in the same way as designers do with product or graphic designs. Problems have to be anticipated through interpreting maps, plans and models. Ideas need to be tested out by means of exhibition and debate.

Strategies

Ideas need to be made external, visible and accessible before they can become the subject for reflection, analysis, discussion and development. It is necessary to express them in order to think, and then to rework, manipulate, extend, and modify them in order to create more complex and refined ideas. There must be some tangible expression of the ideas as a basis for further thought and action. In design, words are not sufficient. The use of a visual language is necessary, with plans, diagrams, maps, drawings and photographs providing a valuable means of understanding the existing situation as well as providing the means to think about change. Photomontage and 3-D models are excellent techniques to try to visualise possibilities for change. Computer-aided design can speed up the process of considering alternatives. It is also necessary to express ideas in order to share them. In organising and managing design activity, it is useful to work in groups, giving individuals a chance to compare ideas, where there is opportunity for negotiation, conflict resolution and compromise. Group work can also benefit from the different perceptions and skills each person brings to the task.

Communication

The work needs to be brought to some kind of resolution or conclusion. Pupils might make booklets or create other forms of documentation. They should be able to present their work in an exhibition or give a presentation, where their work can be discussed. It may be their peers, parents, or other members of the school community who are the 'critical friends'. The results of their work may also be disseminated more widely, to officers in planning departments, elected members or the local press. The techniques that can be used to communicate are also those which the pupils have used to investigate and develop ideas. They include visual, spoken and written means of communication. The form of presentation needs to be appropriate for the audience. Key questions are: What do you want to say? How are you going to say it? Young people should be clear whether they wish to inform, explain or persuade, to explore issues or show alternative possibilities.

Exhibitions

Maps, plans, drawings, photographs, photomontage, models, and cartoons are all media which can be employed in an exhibition to present ideas for environmental change. Exhibitions may be used as part of the consultation or as a means of presenting findings and proposals. They can be used as a focus for discussion and debate at meetings and seminars with different groups. Forms may be prepared to encourage visitors to the exhibition to feed back their comments and ideas. Schools, youth clubs and libraries are obvious venues, but local council officers may also welcome an exhibition of work. Local banks, building societies and other commercial venues might also be interested in displays. Lighting, labelling and security should be adequate and it may be necessary to make arrangements for supervision and maintenance.

Audiovisual presentations

When speaking to a group, it is always useful to have some visual material as illustration. This can act as a visual script, a reminder of what the speaker plans to say. Visual material or text can be transferred to slides or overhead projection acetates. Young people might try out their skills as presenters first on their peers, then on an audience of sympathetic adults before presenting their work to an unknown audience. They should be prepared to react to questions and criticism and for people to object to their ideas. They will need to be able to structure an argument and engage in debate. Adults may have to stimulate discussion and maybe calm things down if discussion becomes overheated.

Leaflets, brochures and booklets

Young people may wish to design newsletters, bulletins, leaflets or brochures for distribution. Presentation and layout of the material is very important here. Is the message clear? Is the text split up to make it more 'readable'? Are there headings and subheadings to help the reader find a way through easily? Who is the targeted readership? Is the material suitably presented? Through the experience of preparing work for a wider audience, young people can see the impact of their ideas on other people. Adults can help by providing feedback and advice, insisting in high standards of presentation, before the work goes 'public'.

Action and implementation

Adults can help young people realise their ideas. They can help them under-stand the complexities of the systems within which they need to operate, including funding and local government planning policy. They can help them gain access to and possibly influence decision-makers. They can create oppor-tunities for them to shape opinion through providing access to the media. They can provide technical support services, so that young people are able to do things they could not do by themselves. They can provide access to funding sources and help them find their way through the bidding system upon which so much of modern life seems to be based. They might extend young people's environmental experience and range of skills by creating opportunities for work experience linked with the environment.

Environmental awareness programme

Young people might organise events such as bulb- or tree-planting, litter picks, a fashion parade with clothes made from recycled materials, an art exhibition at a local library of sculpture made from waste. Seminars and debates on pollu-tion at a school or a stall set up in the local shopping centre to draw people's attention to energy use can form the focus of a day of action. Organising such events can be a complex undertaking. Young people need to decide who will be responsible for the different activities involved and how publicity for the event be arranged. They will have to agree the best time to organise such an initiative and what the programme will involve. They have to be clear what they want to achieve from such an event and how they will be able to use it to publicise their ideas.

Environmental design and development

When groups have developed ideas for environmental change, they will be able to communicate their draft proposals. However, if these are accepted, by the school, the residents' committee or the local authority, there will be a need to translate these ideas into realisable form. There are limits to young people's participation when it comes to the specialised technical knowledge necessary for drawing up plans for implementation by contractors. These will be neces-sary to provide accurate costings, so young people will need help from adults with the appropriate expertise. A development plan will need to be drawn up to programme various activities necessary to make the project happen and fund-raising will probably be necessary. What part can young people play in this phase? Will they be able to contribute to the work in progress, or merely watch it taking place and perhaps record things as they develop? The management of environmental change can be as creative and exciting as formulating proposals for change. It involves thinking about, organising and managing resources, time, costs, people and activities.

To develop the skills necessary to participate effectively in environmental change, young people need to have opportunities to study and appraise their environment, understand the processes which shape it and the systems which control it and gradually learn how they might have an effect on these. The efforts of teachers, community workers, environmental and design professionals working with young people make an invaluable contribution to education for participation.

CHAPTER 14 Facilitating young people's participation

This chapter summarises the current situation and makes ten recommendations for increasing young people's involvement in planning.

This book has described the potential for involving young people in environmental planning. It has shown ways of working and has explained the nature of the relationships involved. It has exemplified partnerships currently operating to support young people's efforts to transform their environment. The work has been dependent upon the efforts of enthusiastic individuals, as well as commitment from local authorities, some of which have been keen to promote young people's participation in planning. Interest in ecological and conservation issues has created concern about the use of resources and an impetus for environmental protection. Added to this, there is now a renewed focus on urban and societal issues relating to quality of life. This points to a need for knowledgeable young people with the appropriate skills to shape and manage their environment and the motivation and confidence to do so.

There is convincing evidence of the potential for developing young people's participation in environmental change. Schools are not the only places where learning takes place and teachers are not the only adults who are responsible for the education of young people. Learning experiences can take place in a range of settings facilitated by different professionals and various people in the local community. To extend opportunities for young people to influence what their environment will be like in the future, we need to consider what adults can do, both as individuals and as members of civic or professional groups, and what schools and government agencies can do, to improve the support systems currently in place at local, regional and national level. The following ten suggestions are made in the hope of stimulating the debate to create strategies for development.

Vision
Enabling young people to participate in environmental change will require a

positive vision of the future, embracing the need for change. It will involve an extension of professional roles, more effective partnerships and the willingness and energy of adults to support the efforts of young people. It is now one hundred years since the Town and Country Planning Association created a vision of a better environment and improved quality of life. How can we help young people create positive and imaginative visions of a future which will result in ways of living in the next century that are sustainable both for the environment and for the communities it supports? Most people live in towns and cities. There is a need to view the urban environment positively rather than as a problem, to understand the urban environment as an eco-system, and to value the complex forms of urban life. All these have implications for the media, for educational publishers and environmental pressure groups.

Access to information

Local authorities generate large amounts of data about the environment. Much of this could be made more readily available to the public. Some of it could be developed as information packs to make excellent educational materials for young people. However, information is not enough. Young people also have to understand the complexities involved and the constraints which have to be taken into account in the process of change. Local authorities may be split into different departments for ease of administration, but people's experience of the environment is not compartmentalised in the same way. Local Agenda 21 may act as a means of linking concerns in different departments. There is a need to identify personnel in local authorities who can liaise between individuals, departments and agencies to create opportunities and develop materials, services and systems to support young people's involvement in environmental planning.

Put it on the agenda

Local authorities could signal their interest and concern for young people by including a regular item on the agenda of planning committees which considered provision for young people in planning matters. How are young people consulted, how are their needs made known, what consideration is there in the planning process to make our towns and cities child-friendly?

Interdepartmental collaboration

Promoting the active involvement of young people in the planning process will require new partnerships between local education authorities, schools, play and recreation units, social services, health services and community organisations. Those with professional expertise will need to take a more proactive stance to engage young people positively and creatively in thinking about environmental change. Interprofessional collaboration between those in the environmental and design professions and those in education and community development will be necessary. Schools will need to reach out and make better use of community agencies. Environmental and education professionals might share training sessions and engage in joint professional development activities.

Figure 19 Young people present their proposals for change in their local neighbourhood to an audience of their peers, teachers, parents and environmental professionals. This is useful preparation for future participation in public meetings

Schools

As we approach the twenty-first century, it is clear that the functions of schools will change to help young people meet the changing circumstances of modern life. The technological revolution, the increasingly rapid speed of change and developments in communication systems mean that schools will probably become very different places. Education will become more important as young people seek to extend their knowledge and skills base to deal with the changes they will inevitably encounter in their lives. More science and technology is not necessarily the answer; they will not solve our problems, merely create new ones. What we do with the knowledge from developments in science and technology is rather more important. Design and planning will take on a renewed significance. Schools will need to give greater attention to cultural and ethical issues of how we choose to live, what it is to be a human being and a member of society.

Community participation

Young people's participation cannot develop in isolation from that of adults. In the UK, public participation is generally seen as adults learning how to say 'no' to development, rather like the two-year-old who is able to exercise some new-found power by constantly repeating that word. The next phase needs to be to extend our vocabulary for participation and perhaps increase our sphere of influence. One suggestion is to make it a requirement that developers of significant projects produce a 'public participation statement' that would identify those affected and set out how they would involve them in the development process (Church, 1996). There could be spin-offs for children and young people, especially where schools or youth groups took an interest and were actively engaged.

Centres

Because of lack of core funding, the architecture workshops and urban studies centres of the 1970s and 1980s are rapidly disappearing. They were appropriate settings for developing skills of participation in the design process and in local decision-making about environmental matters. Some of their work has been taken over by other agencies, but valuable aspects have been lost. If they cease to exist, they will need to be reinvented. What is the potential of the newly created architecture centres in relation to education for participation? How might an effective network of centres be created? Is there a case for 'virtual' environment centres which create new opportunities for consultation and participation? Should local authorities be encouraged to place information about local developments on the Internet? With developments in technology, how might schools themselves evolve in the next century to become centres for participation for all the community?

National focus

Planning and environment are multi-faceted concepts. The physical, social, cultural and economic aspects have to be considered in any programme of environmental change. There are many national agencies concerned with heritage and conservation issues. Others are concerned with environmental and design education. However, there is a need for a greater degree of collaboration between them to ensure a stronger voice for built environment education, to encourage a more positive attitude to urban issues and to think about the changing environment in the future. Effective collaboration between them could also facilitate young people's involvement in planning. A positive start would be to establish a national Built Environment Education Forum which would bring together education, environment and community agencies spanning a range of interests to support education for participation. A key function would be to create a national database, not only of resources and contacts, but as a focus for reporting on and disseminating the results of good practice.

More effective collaboration between the Department for Education and Employment and the Department of the Environment could link curriculum initiatives and planning by ensuring an educational dimension in environmental projects, as well as a more secure place for built environment education in the National Curriculum as part of the current review. A joint initiative funded by the two government departments might also find ways to address the problem of core funding for architecture centres and similar agencies for the long-term development of their education programmes. Long-term development would be possible only if there was a national focus for research and development and an effective means of dissemination and support for professional training. The Teacher Training Agency and the Qualifications and Curriculum Authority will have roles to play here.

International focus

The concern to involve young people in environmental planning and develop the skills and capabilities which will enable young people to participate more fully in the life of their community is not confined to the UK. A glance at the conferences, seminars and workshops held during one month on environmental education across the globe reveals a rich diversity – 'Global Conference on Environmental Education', 'Multidisciplinary and International Cooperation in Environmental Education', 'Children's Participation in Research and Programming', 'Biodiversity and Sustainable Lifestyles', 'European Environmental Education Fair', 'Community and Environment' (*Streetwise*, 1997). However, there is growing danger of fragmentation and marginalisation, of unnecessary divisions between environmental education and development education, between planning for real and education for sustainability. The development of more national associations and councils for environmental education may bring some coherence to the field and will make it easier to establish international connections. The dissemination of information will possibly be made easier by means of e-mail and the Internet. We need to learn from the experience of others and to support education for participation through our own contribution to the wider field.

Individual responsibility

The millennium means that the idea of change and consideration of the future is a common concern. What can we as individuals do in our own practice that will support young people's involvement in environmental planning to engage them in shaping the future? The recommendations made here will not happen unless we accept the responsibility of taking action within our own sphere of influence, whether that be in schools or youth groups, in local authority departments, in the local branch of our professional association or as a citizen lobbying our MP for better education. It will mean that we give more attention to young people's participation in our work as a normal part of our professional practice and are prepared to share the results of our efforts so that others can benefit from our experience.

Hart R. (1997b) 'Children's participation'. *Streetwise* 30, vol. 8, no. 2, July. Brighton: National Association for Urban Studies.

Hehir L. and Kean J. (1992) *Our Built Environment: Design and Technology*. In series 'Interactions, Starting Points, Design and Technology'. Interactions Support Pack. Cheltenham: Stanley Thornes.

Henley Centre for Forecasting (1991). *Young Eyes*. London.

Hicks D. (1994) *Educating for the Future*. Godalming, Surrey: WWF UK.

Hicks D. and Holden C. (1995) *Visions of the Future: Why we Need to Teach for Tomorrow*. Stoke-on-Trent: Trentham Books.

Hillman, M. (1990) *One False Move: A Study of Children's Independent Mobility*. London: Policy Studies Institute.

Hillman, M. (1995) 'The price being paid by children today'. Paper at 'Play in the Streets' Conference organised by the National Children's Bureau, London.

Hogget P. (1995) 'Does local government want local democracy?'. *Town and Country Planning*, vol. 64, no. 4, April, pp. 107–109.

Hood S., Kelley P. and Mayall B.(1996) 'Children as research subjects: a risky enterprise'. *Children and Society*, vol. 10, no. 2, June, pp. 117–128.

IPA Conference (1996) 'Children and Young People'. Thirteenth IPA World Conference, August. Espoo, Finland.

International Institute for Environment and Development (1996) Sustainable Agricultural Programme, Notes on Participatory Learning and Action No. 25.

Jones C. (1995) *Working in Neighbourhoods*. Godalming, Surrey: WWF UK.

Kean J. and Adams E. (1991) *Education for Participation: Local Environment Resource Centres*. Newcastle: Newcastle Architecture Workshop.

Leicester City Council (1995) *The Blueprint Findings*. Leicester.

Local Government Management Board (1996) *Young People and Local Agenda 21*. Roundtable Guidance 4, *Educating for a Sustainable Local Authority*. London.

Longfield J. and Parker N. *Schools and Voluntary Organisations Learning to Work Together*. London: National Council for Voluntary Organisations, Policy Analysis Unit.

Massey J. and Massey M. (1990) *About the Urban Environment*. Cambridge: Hobsons Publishing.

McArthur A. (1995) 'The active involvement of local residents in strategic community partnerships'. *Policy and Politics*, vol. 23, no. 1, pp. 61–71.

Miller A. (1994) *Futuretown, The Town Centre Pack*. London: Venture and Schools Industry Project.

Milson–Fairbairn Report (1969) *Youth and Community Work in the 1970s: Proposals by the Youth Service Development Council*. London: HMSO.

National Association for Environmental Education (UK) and the Royal Town Planning Institute (1995) *The Local Environment in the School Curriculum using Planning Issues, A Guide for Teachers and Planners*. Wolverhampton and London.

National Association for Urban Studies, *Streetwise*, particularly issues 28 (vol. 7, no. 4) and 30 (vol. 8, no. 2).

National Curriculum Council (1990a) *Guidance on Education for Citizenship*. London: School Curriculum and Assessment Authority.

National Curriculum Council (1990b). *Curriculum Guidance 7: Environmental Education*. London: School Curriculum and Assessment Authority.

National Voluntary Council for Children's Play (1995) 'A Charter for Children's Play'. Conference organised in association with the National Children's Bureau, the Child Accident Prevention Trust and Transport 2000, London. November.

National Youth Agency (1995) *Planning the Way: Guidelines for Developing Your Youth Work Curriculum*. Leicester.

Newcastle Architecture Workshop, various reports 1982–1997. Newcastle.

Play-Train (1995) *Article 31 Action Pack: Children's Rights and Children's Play*. Birmingham.

Planning Aid for London (1994) *Planning for the Future. Children Should be Seen and not Heard?* London.

Planning Policy Guidance, note 12 (1992) *Development Plans and Regional Guidance*, February.

Postman N. (1996) *The End of Education: Redefining the Value of School*. Knopf: New York.

Poulton P. and Symons G. (1991) *Eco School*. Godalming: WWF UK.

Renton L. (1993) *The School is Us: A Practical Guide to Successful Whole School Change*. Godalming: WWF UK; DEP (Manchester Development Project).

Rosenbaum M. and Newell P. (1991) *Taking Children's Rights Seriously: A Proposal for a Children's Rights Commissioner*. London: Calouste Gulbenkian Foundation.

Ross C. and Ryan A. (1990) *'Can I Stay In Today Miss?' Improving the School Playground*. Stoke-on-Trent: Trentham Books.

Royal Institute of British Architects (1995) *Teachers and Architects Working Together*. RIBA General Education Group, Symposium Report, October. London.

Royal Society for the Protection of Birds and Council for Environmental Education (RSPB/CEE) (1995) *Our World: Our Responsibility. Environmental Education, A Practical Guide*. RSPB: Bedfordshire; CEE: Reading.

Royal Town Planning Institute (1996) *The Local Delivery of Planning Services*. A summary of the study commissioned from Spawforth Planning and Urban Regeneration Limited, July. London.

Royal Town Planning Institute and National Association for Environmental Education (UK) (1995). *The Local Environment in the School Curriculum Using Planning Issues: A Guide for Teachers and Planners*. London.

Ruse S. (1997) *Children, Young People and the Environment*. A Report of an Action Research Project in Leeds, Leeds Environment City Initiative.

School Curriculum and Assessment Authority (SCAA) (1996) *Teaching Environmental Matters through the National Curriculum.* London.

Skeffington (1969) *People and Planning.* London: HMSO.

Slafer A. and Cahill K. (1995) *Why Design?* Chicago: Chicago Review Press.

Streetwise (1997) Issue 30, vol. 8, p. 2.

Taylor M. (1992) *Citizenship Education in the UK: An Overview.* Slough: National Foundation for Educational Research.

The Children's Society (1994a) *'Ave yer got a minute?* Unpublished internal report. London.

The Children's Society (1994b) *Children should be heard.* Unpublished internal report. London.

The Children's Society (1995a) *Patio Island in the Sun.* Unpublished report on the Patio Project, September. London.

The Children's Society (1995b) *The Needs of Young People, Housing Research in Allerton by the Young People's Project.* Unpublished internal report. London.

Thompson Report (1982) *Experience and Participation: Report of the Review Group on the Youth Service in England*, Department of Education and Science. London: HMSO.

Titman W. (1994) *Special Places, Special People.* Godalming, Surrey: WWF UK.

Town and Country Planning Association, *Bulletin of Environmental Education* 1970s–1980s.

UNICEF (1996) *Children's Rights and Habitat.* Report of the expert seminar convened by UNICEF and UNCHS Habitat, New York, February 1–2.

UNICEF, United Nations Development Programme (UNDP) (1994) *Rescue Mission Planet Earth: a children's edition of Agenda 21.* London: Kingfisher Books.

Uzzell D. (1994) *Children as Catalysts of Environmental Change*, Summary Report. University of Surrey.

Ward C. (1978) *The Child In the City.* London: The Architectural Press.

Ward C. (1995) *Talking Schools*, Ten Lectures by Colin Ward. London: Freedom Press.

Wates N. (1996) *Action Planning: How to use planning weekends and urban design action teams to improve your environment.* London: The Prince of Wales's Institute of Architecture.

White P. (1996) *Spotlight on Children's Rights and the Environment.* First published with Young People Now. London: Save the Children.

Wilcox D. (1994) *The Guide to Effective Participation.* Brighton: Partnership Books.

Willow C. (1997) *Hear! Hear! Promoting Children and Young People's Democratic Participation in Local Government.* London: Local Government Information Unit.

Wylie T. (1996) 'Young People and the Environment', Conference organised by Council for Environmental Education, Reading.

Organisations

Association for Community and Technical Aid Centres (ACTAC)
64 Mount Pleasant, Liverpool L3 5SD

British Trust for Conservation Volunteers
80 York Way, London N1 9AG

British Youth Council
65–69 White Lion Street, London N1 9PP

Children's Rights Office
235 Shaftesbury Avenue, London WC2H 8EL

Civic Trust
17 Carlton House Terrace, London SW1Y 5AS

Community Development Foundation
60 Highbury Grove, London N5 2AG

Council for Environmental Education
University of Reading, London Road, Reading RG1 5AQ

Countryside Commission
P.O. Box 124, Walgrave, Northampton NN6 9TL

English Heritage
23 Saville Row, London W1X 1AB

English Nature
Northminster House, Peterborough PE1 1UA

Groundwork Trust
National Office, 85–87 Cornwall Street, Birmingham B3 3BY

Learning through Landscapes
Third Floor, Southside Offices, The Law Courts, Winchester SO23 9DL

The Local Government Management Board
Layden House, 76–86 Turnmill Street, London EC1M 5QU

National Association for Environmental Education
University of Wolverhampton, Walsall Campus, Gornway, Walsall WS1 3BD

National Association for Urban Studies (Places for People)
c/o ETP, 9 South Road, Brighton BN1 6SB

National Children's Bureau
8 Wakley Street, London EC1V 7QE

National Youth Agency
17–23 Albion Street, Leicester LE1 6GD

National Council for Voluntary Youth Service
11, St Bride Street, London EC4 4AS

Percentage for Participation, RIBA Community Architecture Group
66 Portland Place, London W1N 4AD

Play-Train
31 Farm Road, Sparkbrook, Birmingham B11 1LS

Planning Aid for London
Calvert House, 5 Calvert Avenue, London E2 7JP

Qualifications and Curriculum Authority
(previously School Curriculum and Assessment Authority (SCAA))
Newcombe House, 45 Notting Hill Gate, London W11 3BJ

Rescue Mission: Planet Earth
The White House International Centre, Buntingford, Herts SG9 9AH

Royal Institute of British Architects
66 Portland Place, London W1N 4AD

The Royal Society for the Protection of Birds
The Lodge, Sandy, Beds SG19 2DL

Royal Town Planning Institute
26 Portland Place, London W1N 4BE

Save the Children
17 Grove Lane, Camberwell, London SE5 8RD

Tidy Britain Group
The Pier, Wigan WN3 4EX

Town and Country Planning Association
17 Carlton House Terrace, London SW1Y 5AS

World Wide Fund for Nature (WWF UK)
Panda House, Weyside Park, Godalming, Surrey GU7 1XR

Youth Clubs UK (YCUK)
11 St Bride Street, London EC4A 4AS

Index

The Children's Society

A positive force for change

The Children's Society is one of Britain's leading charities for children and young people. Founded in 1881 as a Christian organisation, The Children's Society reaches out unconditionally to children and young people regardless of race, culture or creed.

Over 90 projects throughout England and Wales

We work with over 30,000 children of all ages, focusing on those whose circumstances have made them particularly vulnerable. We aim to make a real difference by helping to stop the spiral into isolation, anger and lost hope faced by so many young people.

We constantly look for effective, new ways of making a real difference

We pursue new solutions to old problems. We measure local impact and demonstrate through successful practice that major issues *can* be tackled and better resolved. The Children's Society has an established track record of taking effective action: both in changing public perceptions about difficult issues such as child prostitution, and in influencing national policy and practice to give young people a better chance at life.

The Children's Society is committed to overcoming injustice wherever we find it

We are currently working towards national solutions to social isolation, lack of education and the long-term problems they cause, through focused work in several areas:

- helping parents whose babies and toddlers have inexplicably stopped eating, which endangers their mental and physical development;

- involving children in the regeneration of poorer communities;

- preventing exclusions from primary and secondary schools;

- providing a safety net for young people who run away from home and care;

- seeking viable alternatives to the damaging effects of prison for young offenders.

The Children's Society will continue to raise public awareness of difficult issues to promote a fairer society for the most vulnerable children in England and Wales. The Society produces a wide range of publications including reports, books on practice, children's resource materials and national curriculum packs. For further information about the work of The Children's Society or to obtain a publications catalogue, please contact:

The Publishing Department
The Children's Society
Edward Rudolph House
Margery Street
London WC1X 0JL

Tel: 0171 837 4299
Fax: 0171 837 0211